PEOPLE WITH INTELLECTUAL DISABILITIES

Towards a good life?

Kelley Johnson and Jan Walmsley with Marie Wolfe

First published in Great Britain in 2010 by

The Policy Press
University of Bristol
Fourth Floor
Beacon House
Queen's Road
Bristol BS8 1QU
UK

t: +44 (0)117 331 4054
f: +44 (0)117 331 4093
tpp-info@bristol.ac.uk
www.policypress.co.uk

North American office:
The Policy Press
c/o International Specialized Books Services
920 NE 58th Avenue, Suite 300
Portland, OR 97213-3786, USA
t: +1 503 287 3093
f: +1 503 280 8832
info@isbs.com

© The Policy Press 2010

British Library Cataloguing in Publication Data
A catalogue record for this book is available from the British Library.

Library of Congress Cataloging-in-Publication Data
A catalog record for this book has been requested.

ISBN 978 1 84742 068 8 paperback
ISBN 978 1 84742 069 5 hardcover

Cover design by Robin Hawes
Front cover: image kindly supplied by Philip Kearney, KCAT Art & Study Centre, Mill Lane, Callan, Co.Kilkenny, Ireland • www.kcat.ie

Printed and bound in Great Britain by Hobbs, Southampton
The Policy Press uses environmentally responsible print partners.

Contents

Acknowledgements

We would like to thank all of those who have contributed to our thinking and work on this book. Colleagues and friends have supported and challenged us as we worked on the ideas and shaped the chapters. We would particularly like to thank Philip Kearney and the people at KCAT Art & Study Centre, Co. Kilkenny, Ireland for their research and support in providing the art work which is both the cover picture and metaphor for the book. Josephine Flaherty was important in supporting Marie Wolfe and Kelley Johnson in the development of the life history chapter for the book, which is central to its themes. The Social History of Learning Disability group based at The Open University has been a constant source of ideas and collegiality. We would also like to thank the team at The Policy Press for their support and their patience in helping us bring the book to a conclusion.

Introduction: exploring a good life

> We shall not seek from exploration
> And the end of all our exploring
> Will be to arrive where we started
> And know the place for the first time.
> (T.S. Eliot, *Little Gidding*)

This book is an exploration. In it we are revisiting ideas and models that may seem to be familiar territory to those working with or advocating for people with intellectual disabilities and trying to see them again from a different perspective. However, we are also seeking to explore new territory by examining how concepts and theories from outside the disability field or on its margins may contribute new understandings and allow us to think about the lives of people with intellectual disabilities differently.

The end of our exploring is to understand better the nature of 'a good life' and how theoretical constructions of this idea have been played out in the lives of people with intellectual disabilities. We have chosen 'a good life' as a central construct in this book for a number of reasons: it underpins aspirations for all of us in the way we live our lives and philosophers in Western society have explored its possible components for over 2000 years. We know a lot about a good life. However in relation to people with intellectual disabilities it has not really been explicitly central to thinking about their lives. Rather, more modest and, in our view, ill-defined concepts have been used to frame policies and practice. It is salutary to acknowledge that in the UK aspirations and underpinning concepts have been little altered since the publication of the King's Fund's influential *An ordinary life* in 1980. The principles of such a life were spelt out in the Department of Health's *Valuing people* (DH, 2001) as independence, rights, choice and inclusion. The aspiration to achieve an ordinary life was reasserted in December 2007, in the Department of Health's consultation on its Valuing People strategy, *Valuing people now*:

> People with intellectual disabilities want to lead ordinary lives and do the things most people take for granted. (DH, 2007b, p 28)

While concepts of what an 'ordinary life' consists of may have altered since 1980, something we examine in the book, the need to reassert, 28 years later, using the same words, this modest aspiration suggests a failure of implementation. Is an ordinary life a good life? Is it accurately summed up in the words independence, rights, choice and inclusion? Or is there more to it?

While a good life is a central theme in this book we are not providing a recipe for such a life for individuals, although we are conscious that philosophers have at various times attempted to do so. Rather, this concept provides a means of thinking about the current lives of people with intellectual disabilities and the ways in which their lives are constituted by others. The idea of a good life also opens up new possibilities in working with people with intellectual disabilities and allows us to see current and past practices in a different light.

Why this book: beginning the journey

This book developed out of our accumulated experiences and frustrations in working with people with intellectual disabilities as researchers and advocates over 20 years. During that time we have been involved in, and observed, deinstitutionalisation, 'one of the major policy shifts in the last 30 years' (Chenoweth, 2000, p 77) and the movement towards more individualised living in the community by people with intellectual disabilities. We have seen people with intellectual disabilities move from being perceived primarily as 'patients' in need of care and protection to perspectives that see them as citizens with rights. Through the development of the social model of disability in the UK and to a lesser extent in Australia, we have seen an increasing focus on removing social barriers that prevent people with intellectual disabilities from leading fulfilling lives. However, while we have applauded many of these changes, we have become increasingly concerned at the difficulties that many people with intellectual disabilities still experience in living good lives. Personal experience, the findings of empirical research and our reading of disability theory have informed our need to come to a better understanding of why it seems to be so difficult for people with intellectual disabilities to lead a good life, and to make some modest suggestions for thinking about it differently.

Personal experience

Our work with people with intellectual disabilities has raised serious questions for us about the degree to which many people are able to live a good life.

Kelley writes:

> During the past three years I have spent time in a number of different countries working with people with intellectual disabilities. Over that time I met some people who were living in ways that they saw as fulfilling and exciting. However, overall I was left with a sense of frustration and increasing uncertainty about the extent to which changes in legislation and policy have meant changes in the real lives that people with intellectual disabilities lead. The following examples illustrate my anxieties and the questions that arose from them.
>
> In Victoria, Australia, I was a researcher on a large project that was action research-based and was designed to support people with intellectual disabilities to lead good lives in the community after their departure from a large institution (Clement et al, 2006). I spent some weeks observing and participating in one of the community houses to which former institutional residents had gone to live. The physical living conditions of the house, which was in a leafy suburban street, were very good. The house was new, each of the five men living there had a room of their own and there was a large living space. Staff cared physically for the men very well. But the men spent long hours in front of the television and did not participate actively in, or even observe, the work of the household. On excursions into the community it became increasingly clear that they were a presence (sometimes to be avoided by others), not a part of the neighbourhood where they lived (Clement et al, 2006). Was this a good life? Should people be included in the community? None of these men used spoken language and all were physically frail. What would a good life mean to them? How could it be achieved? Should the same policies and practices be attached to this group as to a group of people living relatively independently, able to travel on buses and trains, to work in paid jobs or as volunteers, to develop and sustain relationships without assistance?
>
> In the Republic of Ireland, where I worked for approximately 18 months during 2007 and 2008, changes were happening in many services with an increasing emphasis on individualised

funding and programmes and a slow movement away from institutional life. But in Ireland the Criminal Law Sexual Offences and Crimes Act 1993 forbids people with a 'mental handicap' who are not deemed to be living independently to engage in sexual acts unless they are married. While this legislation has never been tested, its existence has led to concerns among service providers about supporting people with intellectual disabilities to develop relationships or express their sexuality. It has also led to great difficulties for people with intellectual disabilities who may have wanted an intimate or sexual relationship with someone. Does this law support a good life? How important to people are close and intimate relationships? What does this legislation say about the way we see the subjectivity and the desires of people with intellectual disabilities? What is the impact of cultural difference on the lives of people with intellectual disabilities?

In the UK, I worked with people who were strong self-advocates but who had been forced to move from their homes because of bullying and rejection by other people in their neighbourhood: bricks through the window, insults shouted in the street and through the letterbox in the door. In Belgium, a self-advocate spoke of how his life was strictly boundaried between the self-advocacy organisation where he was a leader and other parts of his life where he was perceived as a 'service user' with little power to exercise decision making. Were these good lives? What are the values that underpin the policies supporting community living? How successful have deinstitutionalisation, the social model of disability and social role valorisation been in enabling people to lead good lives in practice?

Jan writes:

Like Kelley, I have felt concerned that legislative, even philosophical, shifts in ideology have not had an impact on the lives of most people. Depressingly, in 2006 and 2007 investigations into practices in two English institutions found abuse that was not unlike that uncovered in the late 1960s and early 1970s in hospitals in England, Wales and in other countries including the USA and Australia (Rivera, 1972; Martin, 1984). We seem to have changed the names we call the places where people live, but we have not changed the attitudes of the staff or the lax management and supervision that allow such practices to flourish (Clement and Bigby, 2010). The low value we accord people with intellectual disabilities appears to be reflected in the low value accorded to the staff who work with them, with manifest gaps in training, in supervision and in working conditions. The result is that, unless staff are exceptionally committed and humane (and many undoubtedly are), there is always a risk of casual disregard for people's humanity behind the inevitable closed doors.

Perhaps, though, these examples were just exceptions to the rule. This book creates a space to consider these experiences and to come to new understandings of what good lives might mean. It is also an opportunity to consider whether a good life is in fact a useful way of thinking about the way people lead their lives.

Research evidence

Personal experiences and frustrations have been strong drivers for us in writing this book, but there are other sources of evidence that new visions and ways of thinking need to be developed. In particular there is now clear evidence, as shown in Table 1 that in spite of the changes to policies and practices over the last 30 years, many people with intellectual disabilities continue to face barriers to living what have been conceptualised as good lives in the community. Table 1, which provides findings from recent research, indicates that many people continue to live in poverty, are unable to access community resources and continue to live isolated and often lonely lives. These figures, taken from the Foundation for People with Learning Disabilities in the UK (www.learningdisabilities.org.uk/information/learning-disabilities-introduction/), are supported by other research evidence (Emerson et al, 2005).

Research evidence from large-scale empirical studies and from the House of Lords/House of Commons Joint Committee on Human Rights (2008) reveals that while the reforms and policy changes have led to the closure of large institutions, in the UK people with intellectual disabilities continue to lead difficult lives. Something does seem to be wrong.

Moving on from current perspectives

We have become concerned at what we see as an inward-looking and static quality to the theories that underpin much of policy and practice in relation to people with intellectual disabilities. We are very aware of the contribution that these ideas and theories have made to the development of change over the past 30 years, but there is a sense

Table I: Statistics and the lives of people with intellectual disabilities[a] in England

Numbers of people

- About 985,000 people in England have a learning disability (about 2% of the population), and 796,000 of them are aged 20 or over.

  (*Estimating future need/demand for supports for adults with learning disabilities in England*, Institute for Health Research, Lancaster University, 2004)

- There are 55,000–75,000 children with a moderate or severe learning disability in England.

  (*Learning disabilities: Facts and figures*, Department of Health, accessed online 2007)

- There are an estimated 210,000 people with severe and profound learning disabilities in England: around 65,000 children and young people, 120,000 adults of working age and 25,000 older people.

  (*Valuing people*, Department of Health, 2001)

Where people with learning disabilities live

- About 60% of adults with learning disabilities live with their families.

  (*Valuing people*, Department of Health, 2001)

- About 39,500 people with learning disabilities live in care homes and hospitals. This is about a third of all the people in touch with learning disability services. About 11,000 of these people live 'out of area', that is away from their home area.

  (*Valuing people – what do the numbers tell us?* Valuing People Support Team, 2005)

Employment and people with learning disabilities

- Seventeen percent of people with learning disabilities who are of working age have a paid job.

  (National Statistics and NHS Health and Social Care Information Centre, 2005)

- About one in 10 people with learning disabilities who are in touch with services is doing any form of paid work.

  (*Valuing people – what do the numbers tell us?* Valuing People Support Team, 2005)

- About one in 20 people with learning disabilities has an unpaid job.

  (National Statistics and NHS Health and Social Care Information Centre, 2005)

Health and people with learning disabilities

- People with learning disabilities are 2.5 times more likely to have health problems than other people.

- Four times as many people with learning disabilities die of preventable causes as people in the general population.

- People with learning disabilities are 58 times more likely to die before the age of 50 than the general population.

  (*Equal treatment: Closing the gap*, Disability Rights Commission, 2006)

- Children and young people with learning disabilities are six times more likely to have mental health problems than other young people.

  (*The mental health of children and adolescents with learning disabilities in Britain*, Institute for Health Research, Lancaster University, 2007)

Friendship and managing one's life

• Over half of people with learning difficulties[a] say someone else decides how much money they can spend each week.

• The friends that people with learning disabilities see most often are friends who also have learning disabilities.

• Almost one in three people with learning disabilities say they do not have any contact with friends. One in 20 have no friends and do not see anyone from their family.

• About a quarter of people with learning disabilities say they would not change what they do in the daytime. Over a third say they would not change what they do in the evening.

• Forty percent of people say they would like more say in what goes on in their everyday life.

• Nearly one in three people said they did not feel safe using public transport.

• Nearly one in three people with learning disabilities said someone had been rude or offensive to them in the last year. In most cases, the person who bullied them was a stranger.

• People with learning disabilities are more likely to have a long-term illness or another disability than other people.

• Only one in four women has ever had a cervical smear.

• More than one in 10 people with learning disabilities say they never feel confident.

Note: [a] In this book the term 'intellectual disabilities' is used (see later discussion about terminology) except for quotations from sources that use alternative terms.
Source: National Statistics and NHS Health and Social Care Information Centre (2005)

in which it has become difficult to develop new ideas and to provide a new approach to existing ones. Sometimes it has felt that ideas simply recycle. Person-centred planning, now at the centre of policy drives to personalise services (DH, 2007a), has been in existence under a variety of names since the 1970s (Blunden, 1980). Individualised funding and budgets were discussed in the early 1990s as Service Brokerage, and have now resurfaced as Individual Budgets or Direct Payments as if they were new, and the solution to all ills.

The social model of disability has been an important impetus for social change, but those who have ventured to offer a critique of its role and place (for example, Shakespeare, 2006) have in turn been roundly criticised for their attempts (see, for example, the reviews of Tom Shakespeare's book in Sheldon et al, 2007). The dialogue, the questioning and the critiques that move us on to new ideas and theories and to different understandings seem to have become muted. We want to revisit the existing theories and ideas and see if there are new ways of exploring them or taking them further.

Normalisation, social role valorisation, deinstitutionalisation, person-centred planning, the social model and, more latterly, personalisation have informed the way in which service providers, policy developers and advocates have shaped the lives of people with intellectual disabilities. All of these perspectives have been advanced as means of increasing the possibility of people with disabilities leading good lives. All of them can provide research that supports their adoption. And all of them are contested by some sectors of the disability community (Shakespeare, 2006).

We recognise the importance of these approaches in promoting a good life for people with intellectual disabilities, but we wonder at the seeming difficulty of managing to achieve this in spite of all the effort. For example, in England the recent government paper, *Valuing people now* (DH, 2009) acknowledged the difficulties of making change happen in spite of the seven years of effort since the last government paper, *Valuing people* (DH, 2001):

> We have seen some good progress in many areas but unfortunately, for far too many people with learning disabilities, little has changed. (Alan Johnson, then Minister of Health, in Foreword to *Valuing people* consultation report, DH, 2007b, p 3)

Over the past three years a number of books and articles have been published that have sought to explore some of these key concepts and models currently relevant to policy and practice with people with disabilities (Shakespeare, 2006; Thomas, 2007; Winance, 2007; Clapton, 2009). While these books provide useful accounts of existing discourses of disability and challenge current positions, they have not really confronted what appears to us to be a major issue: the gap between theory and policy on the one hand, and practice and lived experience on the other. In spite of the many changes that have occurred, research and life histories suggest that many people with intellectual disabilities continue to lead isolated, unfulfilled lives (see, for example, Marie Wolfe's life story in Chapter One of this book and Johnson and Traustadottir, 2005).

The book as an exploration

Some books are written to provide an account of research that has been completed. Others have as their goal a thought-through theory or answer to a problem. This book does neither of these things. It is our attempt to come to grips with a series of questions that are of great concern to us. Through thinking, discussion, reflection and writing, and an exploration of new and old territory, we hope to generate new understandings and new questions.

A number of questions have guided our exploration:

- What meanings have been given to a good life in Western societies? To what extent are the principles of independence, choice, rights and inclusion the underpinnings of a good life in Western philosophical thought?
- What are the implications of the idea of a good life for the lives of people with intellectual disabilities?
- To what extent have current ideas about people with intellectual disabilities been informed by wider thinking about a good life?
- Can and should all people with intellectual disabilities lead the same kind of 'good' life?
- What values relevant to defining a good life underpin current disability theories, ideas and discourses?
- What contribution have they made to the lives of people with intellectual disabilities?
- How well have the theories been translated into practice by those who work with people with disabilities?
- What are their implications for the way we describe and constitute groups of people who are labeled disabled?
- Are there new ways of thinking about good lives for people with intellectual disabilities?
- What are the implications of values and theories for those working with people with disabilities?

While these questions focus on the issues affecting a 'good life' for people with intellectual disabilities we believe that they are also relevant to other groups regarded as 'excluded'. Notions of what constitutes a good life underpin many government policies and practices. Achieving a 'good life' has been one of the catch cries for older people, for people living with chronic illnesses and for those with mental health issues. While recognising differences between these groups, we also think that many of our questions may be relevant to them.

Who might use this book? Fellow travellers

Like our previous jointly authored book (Walmsley and Johnson, 2003), this one is an attempt to create space to reflect on our own practice and experience as well as to generate new understandings that may be useful to others. It is not a book designed to be used directly by people with intellectual disabilities, although we hope that some parts of it may be useful to them. We have written the book to challenge the values, the expectations and the ideas of those who exercise power over the lives of people with intellectual disabilities or other marginalised groups.

We aim to provide a means by which unquestioned assumptions and values can be analysed and critically examined. We anticipate that the book will be particularly useful to those who work directly with, or try to support, people with intellectual disabilities as paid service providers/staff, as advocates, as family and as friends. However we also hope that it may be relevant to policy development and to generating theory in the disability field.

We have particularly addressed this book to those, like us, who have been struggling with the gap between hopes and aspirations and the reality in relation to how people with intellectual disabilities live their lives. And we are hoping to engage with those who want to look at things differently. We hope our book will be a dialogue between us and our readers and provide a space for new kinds of discussions and action.

A word on terminology

We have used the term intellectual disabilities throughout this book because it is increasingly recognised internationally. This might open us to criticism because the language we use for this emotive topic creates great debate. Our view is that labels are often problematic for the people who are subject to them. This is particularly the case with intellectual disabilities, which is now an umbrella term applied to an extremely diverse population.

While uncomfortable with the label, we have after all set out to write a book that explores issues affecting the lives of people with intellectual disabilities. We are therefore a part of the labeling process. Labels are often devaluing or demeaning, but they can also act as a signal for specific needs and desires of individuals or a group. We hope that our book primarily reflects the latter function. We also hope to challenge current views of the nature of the 'group' of people labeled as having intellectual disabilities.

The nature of the journey

This book is divided into three parts. The first part is concerned with reflecting on a good life. It begins, in Chapter One with an account by Marie Wolfe, a woman with intellectual disabilities, of her search for a good life. Marie's life story begins this section because it provides a grounded microcosm of many of the themes we wish to explore and it also illustrates graphically the difficulties and the triumphs of this search by one woman.

Chapter Two explores how a good life has been constituted at different times and in different places. Philosophers, politicians and social theorists among others have attempted to come to some definition of a good life over thousands of years. And at an individual level we would argue that we each attempt to find our own version of a good life. This chapter does not attempt to provide a detailed account of the nature of 'a good life'. To do so would involve the development of a book (or a library) in itself. Rather it seeks to provide some glimpses of how we might think about a good life and the way in which definitions of it are framed by time and place. It then explores the values that seem to underpin the good life in the 21st century in many of the 'developed countries'. The chapter examines in particular the increasing tension between the idealisation of community and the increasing focus on individualism in these societies. The latter focuses on issues of independence and autonomy as key ingredients in the contemporary 'good life'.

In the final chapter in this part of the book, we reflect on the implications of how a good life has been constituted in Western societies for people with intellectual disabilities. This chapter explores how our views of a good life inevitably seem to exclude some groups of people from the possibility of living one. We argue that the prevailing dominant discourse in our society leaves out many groups of people for whom the values that inform current policy are not achievable and are largely irrelevant. This chapter explores the way in which some groups are identified within society as outside the parameters of achieving 'the good life'. While the chapter focuses on people with intellectual disabilities we argue that other groups who have emerged as 'categories' during the 20th century may also find themselves struggling to conform to wider societal concepts of a good life. These groups include people labeled as having autism, long-term health issues or mental health issues such as dementia. The chapter concludes that efforts to create 'good lives' through policy and practice are constrained by the ways in which the very concept of a good life has been conceived in our societies and by the ways people who have been given the label of intellectual disability are seen by others . In particular we challenge the view that people with intellectual disabilities constitute one group to whom a unitary conception of a good life can apply.

Part Two, 'Re-examining concepts in the light of current practice', takes as its themes the strengths and limitations of prevailing conceptual models as a framework for delivering improved lives for people with intellectual disabilities. Its key argument is that the dominant theoretical frameworks of the late 20th century, which have been developed and applied to practice in this field, provide only part of the answer to the impoverishment of the lives of people with intellectual disabilities.

Chapter Four, 'A good life in policy', traces the emergence of ideas about a good life in policy. It seeks to deconstruct some of the conceptual and theoretical perspectives that have framed the search for a good life. In particular it is concerned with the values that underlie each of these conceptualisations and their links to ideas of what makes a good life. It considers the contributions of key theories – normalisation, social role valorisation and the social model of disability – to current policy, and how people with intellectual disabilities and the organisations that represent them have expressed their aspirations for a good life.

Chapter Five, 'Changing discourses', examines the different ways the problem presented by intellectual impairment has been framed, and the different solutions adopted. In the early 20th century the problem was the threat posed by the 'feeble-minded', the solution was their control in institutions or surveillance in the family. After the Second World War, the problem was reframed as the threat to family life posed by 'mental handicap', 'subnormality' or 'retardation'. The solution was 'community care', with the family idealised as the model for a 'good life'. If families were unavailable, then the 'good life' was to be recreated in 'family-type' settings – in the 'community'. Our current framing of the problem is that there has been a denial of opportunities and supports to live a good life, premised on ideas of independence, choice, rights and inclusion. The solution was individualised budgets, paid work, single-person tenancies with personalised support, and the dismantling of those segregated settings created under 'community care'. The chapter argues that over the 20th century we have moved from an exclusion of people regarded as unequal under the social contract to theoretical inclusion of these people within this framework.

Chapter Six, 'Changing constructions of work', is a case study of an important policy goal, the centrality of paid work, the ultimate badge of citizenship and inclusion. It traces the different ways work has been constructed for people with intellectual disabilities.

Part Three of the book explores how ideas about a 'good life' that have their origins outside the intellectual disability field may be used to change the way we think about how a 'good life for people with intellectual disabilities can be achieved. We examine this in three ways: through considering rights (Chapter Seven), community and inclusion (Chapter Eight) and independence (Chapter Nine). This builds on our earlier analysis of a good life and is premised on the view that independence, rights, choice and inclusion, the values or principles that explicitly underpin current policy, oversimplify the challenges of finding a good life. In particular, they can all too easily lead to the imposition of a good life on people without taking account of their histories, feelings and need to belong. For example, the stress on 'independence' may impose unrealistic expectations on people who will inevitably rely, to a greater extent than everyone else does, on others; 'inclusion' can all too easily be interpreted as 'insertion' (Winance, 2007) into situations where people will always struggle.

People with intellectual disabilities are not one group with identical needs. Chapters in this part of the book explore how ideas from outside the disability field may be used by people with very different support needs and by those who work with them.

The third and final chapter in this part examines how relationships are pivotal to people with learning difficulties leading a good life. It argues strongly that workforce development and training are neglected areas of current concern, in part because of the way we have constituted a good life for people with intellectual disabilities. This chapter explores how the ideas of relationships in the community can be used in the field of intellectual disability.

The conclusion revisits the philosophical ideas that underpin our relationships with each other as citizens. It then argues that there is a need to move beyond a myopic or inward-looking approach of disability to a readiness to explore ideas and theories from outside the field in order to inform new ways of working and viewing the nature of intellectual disability.

Conclusion

This book has been an exploration for us. It provided us with an opportunity to rethink some long-held assumptions and beliefs. Reading for this book has engaged us with a number of theoretical perspectives that were new to us and we have in a very real sense 'written ourselves' into new understandings. We hope that the readers of this book will find the ideas in it challenge conceptions and lead to new ideas and practices. Most importantly we hope that the book may contribute to supporting people with intellectual disabilities to lead 'good' lives.

Part One
Reflecting on a good life

In this part of the book we address the following three questions outlined in the Introduction:

- What meanings have been given to a good life in Western societies?
- What are the implications of ideas about what constitutes a good life for the lives of people with intellectual disabilities?
- Can and should all people with intellectual disabilities lead the same kind of good life?

ONE

My own life

Marie Wolfe with Kelley Johnson

Marie Wolfe's life story is the story of one woman's striving to define and achieve a good life on her own terms. We use it throughout the book as a reference point.

Kelley writes:

I met Marie through Josephine Flaherty who is both her friend and support worker. Marie wanted to tell her life story, but she wanted Josephine to be there as she told it. We met three times over 12 months. The first time we met in a hotel in Galway and talked about doing a life story and Marie talked a little about her life as it was then. The second time we met at my home in Dublin. The third time was again in Galway at Marie's apartment. There was a lot of talk between Marie and Josephine as we went along but this is Marie's story and so I have not included Josephine's contributions directly. Over the 12 months, Marie's life changed a great deal. I have sometimes changed the tense of the verbs so that the story makes sense to the reader. One of the things that was very important to Marie was her concern with justice for people with disabilities and the importance in her life of being an advocate. So in some parts of the story I have included her comments on what a particular[1] part of her life has meant in terms of other people.

> "I like it when I don't have people telling me what to do kind of. My own life. When I am my own boss. That's how I like it. Just having my own space like you know. Sometimes it can get a bit annoying if you don't have enough to do kind of.
>
> "I would like to keep doing the work I am doing and keep doing what I am doing. As long as I can. And as long as I am helping somebody I am happy. As long as somebody gets something out of it I am happy you know."

Being an advocate

"My dream is to keep going and help people as much as I can, that's all I want to do, and keep being here in my flat, that's my dream.

"The self-advocacy group Josephine started meant a lot to me. It was kind of something I could speak up about. All those people with me you know. [It began] I think it was in 1996. We went to People First self-advocacy group in the UK.

"Josephine pushed me I think, and that was good. You know what I mean? Gave me more ideas, stretched me a bit.

"Then [later] I became a member of the National Advocacy Council. I was elected as representative from Galway. We meet four times a year in Galway and we meet with the director of Brothers of Charity in Galway. Then the national council meets for four days with the national Director of Brothers of Charity. The issues need to be on the agenda to be discussed.

"We have a conference. We started the first national conference in Galway in 96. It was really good.

"[I was chairperson of the National Council.] I resigned. I think I wanted to take a break. Then I came back. I was really committed to it. I could have taken a full-time job a couple of years ago but I didn't do it. I stayed committed to [the Council], and I stayed going to the meetings and everything even though I could have done more with my life. I could have, but I stayed with them you know.

"Later I did get a job. And it [stopped me being on the] National Council. I had to take a back seat kind of. And I have missed a year now. I haven't been able to go. I think I have had a back seat. Really for the last year."

Thinking about others

"There is something that I would like to say. I would like people to have a life like I have, get more support, get out there, do more, get more meaningful jobs. Get experience you know. Do a trade, learn skills.

"I think people have to stand up for themselves in a right way. People have to give support like. People have to be open more. And be a bit more understanding. But before you actually move out to get a place there should be some kind of training something out there.

"I wouldn't say I had training like.

"With money like you can get into debt as well. There's training there."

Family

"I have a good relationship with my parents. At the beginning, I didn't like them you know. They learned to let me go now, kind of. The only thing is [they still say] 'Did you lose weight and all?', but that's the only thing, like. But I'm kind of tackling that myself, I'm at Weight Watchers. But that's the only thing, the odd mention, like.

"They even said to me once: 'You might get married.' It [surprised me] like. As long as I seem to be getting on well, they keep out of it. They don't really talk to any staff or anything they don't interfere or anything. It's good, like. Not many parents are like that, you know.

"[I have] two brothers. They are younger [than me]. There is only a year and half between me and Desmond. My other brother, Patrick, he's a marine engineer and he's actually hoping that he will be a qualified engineer. Sometimes I wish that Patrick could have helped me a bit more in my life you know. Just come over for a cup of tea the odd time. He's a bit closer to me now. But they've got their own lives to lead like. You don't want them too close."

Growing up

"[I was in England] when I was a child. It wasn't too bad like. I can't remember that far [back]. But I can remember when I was at the swimming pool and I used to go there for a swim and I met these people and I was still 13 and I got into a fight and they punched me nose or something. I [just] took it. The best way.

"I thought they were my friends but I was young then. I was a bit naïve. After that my parents got protective kind of. Like one time I met these people in the park and I thought they were my friends and they said they were going to a disco and I said to mum 'Can I go to the disco?' She said 'No no it's not right you know. Dangerous.' And I tried to go and they said 'No'.

"I went to a special school because I had a learning disability. Back then that was the way to do it. I think I have more opportunities now than I had back then you know. I left when I was about 13 or 14. I went to another school. I think towards the end I moved to a kind of college. At school I learned how to treat people with respect like.

"One of the memories of when I was young [was] this girl got smacked at school. It was back when I was about 7 or 8 she got smacked. The headmistress just smacked her. God I didn't like it like.

"And another thing I remember when I was at school. We used to visit this other school and I started writing a letter to somebody I really liked I had a crush on. Mum found the letter and she really didn't like it. My parents were a bit old-fashioned and they still are about things like that.

"I used to play with my brothers. I used to play with my Sindy dolls.

"I used to dress them up and comb their hair and wash their hair like and all things like that.

"I had a few [friends] but I didn't have that many friends. [I lost them] when we came to Ireland.

"I was 17 when we moved to Innismore in Ireland. I didn't have a choice [about coming to Ireland]. It was a bit boring when I moved to Innismore first. There's about a thousand and a half people on the island but there's more in summer kind of. But not much to do really. When I was in Ireland I kind of helped with the business and things. I was helping mum with the garden and things and the restaurant. It was boring. You need a purpose in life really. I'm not surprised I kind of had a breakdown when I did because there was probably not much else to satisfy my needs really."

Towards a good home

"At one point I had a breakdown when I moved from London to Aran in Ireland. My mum kind of couldn't manage me. It was a hard time. I was in hospital then. And from hospital I went to the Brothers of Charity when I was 21.

"When I came out of hospital, I went into a group house. It wasn't the best thing really for me. It was terrible. Same dinners all the time every week, the same time, like, you didn't feel it was your house. Like you couldn't really make a cup of tea when you wanted. That was back then anyway. The staff did all the cooking and everything. [I had no choice about the people I lived with.] They weren't the people I wanted really you know. They'd different interests kind of.

"It wasn't a lot of change [from living at home], but at that point you know, I didn't know much about advocacy and rights at all really I didn't know that I had rights really. I was a lot shyer anyway, a lot quieter.

"Later [I moved into a flat next door to the group house]. It wasn't really the flat that I'd choose, you know. See, back then the staff used to come in, in the evening. It still was controlled really. I was doing a steak one day and she [staff] said 'What are you cooking that for?' It wasn't independent living, as you'd call it.

"Then I moved to an apartment in Galway. Two bedroom apartment. Next to my place there was a place for cars to park. There was no actual garden. It was good.

"To Christine [my flatmate] it was small, but it was alright, like. But I wanted a one-bedroom apartment. I thought 'It's time [to be alone]'. It suited me when I moved in first, like. It did, like. Compared to some places where people live with disability. Like living in garages, no heat or anything. So it suited me.

"There was no way [of living alone]. There was going to be another girl but I thought she wouldn't be suitable. So we thought of Christine. [We lived together] nearly two years. I'd known her before. We went to a few things. Holidays. Conferences. I thought it'd be nice to give her a chance. We did get on, but sometimes she kinda had a different approach to things. When she is right you can't argue with her, like. She's just a different manner, but deep down she is a nice person. With Christine I can see a person rather than a disability. And I think I gave her a chance, really. [We are] different personalities. I kinda got used to her. And whatever she says I just stand up to her and sometimes I say to myself:

'Don't argue with her. Just let it go,' and I have to put my point in. We seemed to get on okay, really. We didn't involve staff, or anybody and we kept it that way, and I think that's good. We sorted it out ourselves.

"Last December 8th I moved into my new apartment in Jahiscka by myself. It's with the rental scheme. It's private rented and I'm by myself kind of. Oh I do like my own company. I switch on the box. Like I have a digital TV. So it's not too bad. I watch lots of things on it. I am kind of used to watching TV now. I won't say that I go out that much you know. Maybe once a week maybe on Saturdays.

"Christine's next door to where we were living before. We see each other we ring each other on the phone. We go out to the clubs and things together. She's a bit different to me and sometimes if you ring her you can get kind of a bit thrown off sometimes. I think she's a bit better than my other friend Anne Marie like. When she stays she can't go to the night clubs. Her mother won't let her. But I can go. I wouldn't go by myself. I go with Christine. But isn't it funny? I think she likes the quieter places. She likes Park House [a hotel on the square] and I kind of like Cuba and clubs more.

"It would be nice to have a volunteer sometimes. Somebody young. But somebody fun like. [She] could maybe go out. Like on Friday or Saturday every week maybe with Christine and me."

My fear

"They say you don't know what the future holds, nobody does really, but I'd rather, I'd rather be dead than be in a group home that's the way I feel. Dependent on other people to take you to the toilet and it's not that I want. Or telling you when to go to the toilet, or things like that, showering you, that's not what I want from life. I never want to be like that. Never. I'd rather be dead. I don't want that life. It's just not for me. You just feel you're nobody, no life, you're not recognised. People will do everything for you. It's not me so I always worry. I always have that on my mind, you know. If my memory got worse I'd have to go back, there's nothing anybody could do. I'd just go back, you know, if I deteriorate you know, if I got cancer, if my memory did start going I'd have to go back you know, I just don't want to."

Thinking about others

"When people are in institutions [and then leave they need help] because it's like their lives starting all over again. They've been in the institution 20 or 30 years they're going to live their life again and they're going to need help. Like they're going to have to learn all over again how to do things, like. And it's like when some people come out of group homes and come into independent living some of them just go off and drink too much, and they're back in. See there needs to be support, there needs to be some support there. It's hard like, they might go off the rails. It's quite hard, they need therapy as well. They need advocacy there. There needs to be some kind of training, when they move out of institutions, you know.

"I think staff need training to be more confident, you know, and to speak the right way to me, you know, 'cos some of them can be a bit bossy you know. I think they need to really put their feet in my shoes, kind of.

"Another thing that's come to me is people being moved house to house, and sometimes they move them to areas that are away from shops and everything, there's no parks, and it just makes them upset, and then what happens is they're swapped from one [house] to the other, and the staff are thinking 'Why are they getting upset?'

"Well, course they're getting upset. They're moved with some people they don't know or don't get on with."

Finding a good job

"[In England] for a while I had a few jobs cleaning houses. I did it by myself. I think I had a job two hours a week or something.

"[While I lived in the group house] I went to the centre most days like. Doing tips and things. Putting them into little, kind of boxes, and you put them into little holes. We did it for companies or something. [I didn't get paid for that.]

"And then a couple of years after that, I think it was '98, I started working in the garden centre next door [to the group home]. I worked there kind of, but working in the garden centre wasn't what you'd call the ideal thing to be doing. It was boring I thought. I remember watering plants and things like that. I don't think I was really suited to what they had, you know. Wasn't my piece of cake anyway. I didn't get paid.

"[No one asked me what I wanted to do.] I suppose I didn't know myself. Really I didn't. You know they didn't come and ask me 'Would you like to do this?' and you know sit me down and [talk].

"[When I moved to Galway from the group house] I was a year out of work doing nothing. A year. I slept a lot. It was hard, the year I was out like, it kinda felt like, like least now you know you get up for something, but before it was kinda, there was no boundary, it was kinda like you'd no life and Mum and Dad would ask 'What are you doing?' and when I went over to the centre sometimes to pay my rent they'd ask 'What are you doing?' People, everybody was asking 'What are you doing?' and why I wasn't at work, like. But it wasn't my fault, like. I still went to meetings. Oh and I was in Blue Teapot, at that time I was in Blue Teapot [drama group]!

"[Josephine] managed to drum up enough things for me to do, but it wasn't nice, you know. I'd no confidence either. I was on my own. One thing I noticed about when I was in the service, when I wasn't doing anything staff wouldn't tell me off and say 'You have to do something,' you know. They always left me alone. It's like they wouldn't say anything to me 'cos they're scared. They let me do what I want. Kind of they wouldn't say 'Go off to the centre,' or 'Go off to summer training.'

"[Then] Josephine saw an ad in the paper. And she brought it to me, and then I rang up. I applied for [the job] and I went for an interview and I got it. I think that was the right job for me then. I was in Failté house [community employment scheme] for two years. I was in reception. I got to know the other staff as people, you know. I got to know the person rather than what they looked like. But there could have been a bit more support from my boss. When I was let go at Failté house I felt like they could have kept me on. There's a lady who works at the office and she always is inviting me when they have parties, like the Christmas get-together, I'm always welcome at tea break, probably the only one who's invited. Sometimes I kind of think it would have been nice if I stayed there. Sometimes I look at my life. Sometimes even now [I think] 'Should I be doing more, like?' I don't know.

"Then I worked in Scotty's, part time for about 12 months. It's a café. They're from America. I would wash up, put stuff into the dishwasher, clear tables and ask when I go to each table: 'Would you like me to take any plates?' and I took them. But I kind of would ask them and I kind of just, not talk too much, you know. If there were people that come in I'd say 'Hello, how you doing?' you know.

"It could get busy from 1–2, like. Mostly 1–2 [o'clock] but sometimes it could be manageable like but you had to expect it to get busy, anyways. Ah, it wasn't too bad, like.

"You have to work for it really you know to get money, kind of thing. Everything can't be a piece of cake, like you know. I kind of did up to about 12.5 hours a week. I wished it had been more. I would have liked more. We asked but I didn't get more. It was nice to work like you know. They were very good, like, you know. And I think I was the only person out of the whole lot that had a learning disability, I think so. It was good being the only one, like, you know.

"I knew some of them [the other staff] like, but I tried not to get involved in the staff issues or whatever, you know. But I seemed to get on with them. I was nice to them. You have to be polite to people, you know. I didn't see them [out of work].

"Sometimes I thought, like, 'Should I be working with food?' I was, like, 'Should I be working in a restaurant?' I'm a people person. I liked the job for a while. It was kind of, I s'pose, different you know?

"Then I left. I didn't know I was going to leave. It was on my mind but I didn't [go]. I stayed you know. I think that was the wrong job for me totally. I'm not domesticated.

"Scotty's was not satisfying my needs you know. I mean in spite of everything they were nice people but it wasn't enough hours really."

"I just [wanted] to be more busy. I was told at the beginning it would be 12-and-a-half hours a week.

Sometimes [I only worked] for an hour a day. Sometimes it was two hours. One week it was two days. There was no point in them having me on when they didn't need me.

"[Leaving my job at Scotty's was hard.] People probably think you should stay there and everything. And people said 'Oh Marie she's great, she's got a job.' And then they said 'Well what do you want to change that job for?' But it wasn't right for me. And it's about, I think, rights, you know?

"I think I did the right thing I really do think I did the right thing but some people may not think that. We all have different opinions like.

"They're [the employment service] looking for another job for me. But see the last time I went to see her she said 'You don't really know what you want. You need to write down on a piece of paper what you want and you don't want'. She said 'You don't know what you want' and maybe I don't know what I want. Maybe go back to college or something. Not sure of that one really.

"People probably think 'Oh you've got a job, that's fine' but that isn't what I want, really you know. I think it's time to do something different, completely different, you know."

Dreams of work

"[My dream job] would be something to do with conferences, kinda speaking at conferences. But like you couldn't really have that for a job and I'm not great for travel – I couldn't travel by myself to other countries. There wouldn't be enough conferences really. I wouldn't do it by myself. Some people can do it by their self, I'm sure there's people in London who are doing that like. But having a support worker or something I wouldn't mind.

"Something to do with advocacy or I'll speak at the college and speak to people about rights and about disability. I wouldn't like to do it as a career, just as a hobby.

"I would like to do some modelling. Be lovely to do a modelling weekend in London or something. Model, do fashion shows or something like that, I'd love it. I'm a bit of a queen. But I don't know if they have people as big as me in fashion shows.

"And I've always loved singing, even though I'm not a brilliant singer, but I've loved that. I love going to karaoke. Anyway, I'd love to do that maybe next year.

Towards love and relationships

"In the group homes people never got opportunities to express their feelings or thoughts. You see, some of them in the group homes don't get a chance. It's like they are under 24 hour watch!

"If you're in the services now, and you have a crush on somebody, it's so hard that a lot of them can't talk to anybody about it, you know. And that's where advocacy comes into it.

"While you're in group homes, I doubt staff will [allow relationships]. They have to be [accountable] if somebody would get pregnant. So it means that [the person] would really have to move. If they really wanted to have a boyfriend, or something, they'd have to move out. They shouldn't have to move out, I know. That's the thing, they should be accommodated for, like.

"But imagine being in a group home with a boyfriend, it wouldn't probably work would it?

"I kind of imagine sometimes having a relationship. I like a bit of fun, flirting and all that. If you have a boyfriend he knows other people and that would open doors for you.

"My mum said to me 'Would you like to have a child?' And I was like 'No no!' She said to me, 'Would you ever get married or anything?' And I said 'No, no', I'm happy the way I am, you know.

"I haven't [ever been in love]. But I thought 'Would I ever get that chance in life?' You never know. You know you fantasise about these things, I'd like to have the opportunity but … you never know I'm very changeable. There has been, like, when I was younger I had a crush. When I was 13, 14 I had a crush on this teacher at school. And never saw him since, that was a long time ago. And then when I went to college I had a crush on somebody. He was a teacher. And I knew it couldn't go anywhere, but like it was hard at the time. I couldn't say anything. He was funny, you know, I was a bit flirty you could say. But I think he thought I was very good at what I know. It was just fun, you know. We all go through that. There's nothing in it really, like you know. I know nothing can ever come of it, still sometimes I look back and think of that time, you know. A lot of it is fantasy, you know. It's, you know nothing could never come of it, that's how I look at it. He's married and he's children, so that's the end of that."

Thinking about other people

"And another thing, people with severe learning difficulties, they could have a relationship, not a sexual relationship but somebody close.

"They don't have anything, they don't have anybody close, they could have a slight relationship couldn't they? It's sad.

"I think all services in Ireland need to be more open to relationships, because it's the way things are moving on, it's the way the world is.

"It's a human rights thing. That's a right, that's a basic right. They're taking their rights.

"We should run workshops about this."

The things I like

"Sometimes I go into town, kind of after work to pass the time and then sometimes I get home after 5 and then I watch television, so I do find recently, like, 'Where is my life going?' Sometimes I do find that.

"I do a lot of cooking. I do like cooking. I'd rather on a weekday cook than eat out, like. I can do lamb chops and things, spaghetti bol. I'm not a brilliant cook like my Mum, but.

"I like singing in karaokes. I thought I was a great singer, but when I heard other people in the Brothers of Charity, other people with learning disability, I'm alright but I find I've awful trouble with the words. My voice isn't that strong. My mum can sing too, so it's in the family.

"I like shopping, looking at things, like. I like clothes, wearing clothes. I thought one time I'd like to be a model but I think it's too hard work. I think you have to be a lot thinner for a model, but I don't think that's me really. I'm kind of a people person.

"I like films, yeah. I like films that people have disabilities in. I watched *Jane Eyre*. It was brilliant. It's a love story. It was brilliant. She fell in love and whatever. And when I was watching it, I said to myself, 'Will I ever get that chance in life?'"

Towards a better life?

"I just want life to get better. I know sometimes things will never get better but there is probably a reason why things happen in life, you know. Hopefully the stronger I'm getting, doing more things, people will see.

"I think also some people admire me. I forget things sometimes, but I get on with my life and that's something. You could be going to the doctor, going to the staff and saying, 'I forget this,' you know, and you could be complaining and going on. But there's not much they can do, you have to just keep moving on. I'm sure some people have seen me managing. I think sometimes I'm an inspiration to people like. You can either go one way in life – can either go down or you can go up."

Note
[1] This chapter would not have been possible without the help of Josephine Flaherty, Marie's friend and support worker.

TWO

Thinking about a good life

"I like it when I don't have people telling me what to do kind of. My own life. When I am my own boss. That's how I like it. Just having my own space like you know. Sometimes it can get a bit annoying if you don't have enough to do kind of.

"I just want life to get better. I know sometimes things will never get better but there is probably a reason why things happen in life, you know. Hopefully the stronger I'm getting, doing more things, people will see.

"They say you don't know what the future holds, nobody does really, but I'd rather, I'd rather be dead than be in a group home that's the way I feel. Dependent on other people to take you to the toilet and it's not that I want." (Marie Wolfe)

Marie's search for a good life includes many of the ingredients that we commonly see as underpinning a good life: independence, a sense of ownership of her own life, a need for close and intimate relationships and meaningful work. But her attainment of these elements of a good life is fraught with difficulties and remains precarious, threatened by her view of her own fragility and the power exercised by others over her. Where did her view of a good life come from? Why is it so elusive? In this chapter and the next, we explore some of the ideas and theories that underpin Marie's view of what a good life is.

More particularly, in this chapter, we address the first of the questions that frame this book: what meanings have been given to a good life in Western society? Over the past few years there has been a number of published books in which the authors have tackled the meaning of a good life from different disciplinary perspectives and with different emphases. These books have examined the relevance of past conceptions of a good life to the present (see, for example, Cottingham, 1998; de Botton, 2001; Grayling, 2003, 2007; Russell, 2005; Eagleton, 2007; Bauman, 2008; Kohn, 2008). While this literature may seem far removed from Marie's lived experience we would argue that it is relevant to understanding both her life and those of other people with intellectual disabilities who are the subjects of this book.

Historically a good life has been explicitly defined in relation to certain groups of citizens. The Greek philosophers did not include women or slaves as citizens and they were not included in a view of the good life that was based on what was then seen as a man's province: reason. Gradually, though not without problems, the idea of a good life has been developed to include some groups, such as women, who were formerly excluded. It is only in recent times that a good life has been consciously sought by, and for, disabled people. The links between the ways a good life is thought about in the broader society and how it is then explored in relation to people with intellectual disabilities were unclear to us and form the motivation for this chapter, which aims to address four questions:

1. Why is it important to look at the wider ideas of a good life in relation to people with intellectual disabilities?
2. What are some of the ways that we have given meaning to a good life for human beings in Western societies?
3. To what extent have current ideas about people with intellectual disabilities been informed by wider thinking about a good life?
4. What are the implications of these meanings in relation to people with intellectual disabilities?

Addressing these questions took us on an exploration of ideas that lie outside the field of disability. It has been an exciting journey. In this chapter we share some of the ways in which philosophers and other writers have tried to understand this nebulous concept, which is central to the way we live our lives. From the reading, discussion and thinking involved in preparing the book a number of important themes emerged. All of these have implications for how people with intellectual disabilities and other marginalised groups live in our society.

There are two caveats to this chapter. Our exploration is Eurocentric in nature although we believe that we could learn a great deal from the different conceptions of a good life that a broader cultural perspective could offer. In part our emphasis was shaped by the need to examine what was happening in the societies to which we both belong. In part it was lack of time that prevented us from engaging with such a large body of literature; Eastern philosophy, for example, which we know would have offered very different conceptions of a good life.

Further, the analysis we offer is not one embedded in the discipline of philosophy, to which neither of us belong. We make no apologies for this. Our exploration was done for a specific purpose. We have sought to identify from our reading and thinking, some themes and ideas that seem to inform the ways that a good life has been constituted. We offer the ideas that we have gleaned as a starting point and throw the challenge to our readers to deepen, endorse, criticise and add to our contribution.

Why is it important to consider the idea of a good life in relation to people with intellectual disabilities?

When we began this book it was not our intention to become involved in an exploration of the nature of a good life more generally, although we were interested in looking at the possible contribution of disciplines outside of the disability field to new ideas about how people with intellectual disabilities might more easily lead one. We were concerned most particularly with why it seemed so difficult for people with intellectual disabilities to gain access to what many others in the society took for granted. However as we began to work on the book the need to explore the idea of a good life more generally became increasingly important.

Many of the policies that governments have developed over the past 20 years, and which have sought to guide services and to support people with intellectual disabilities, were premised on concepts that did not explicitly focus on a good life. Rather they have used terms such as an 'ordinary life' or a 'valued life' or a 'life like any other'. There appear to be a number of assumptions underlying these policies. Perhaps implicitly there is an assumption that there is already a consensus on what a good life might mean for people with intellectual disabilities and that this does not need to be conceptually spelled out, but will be revealed in the specific provisions of policies. This has not always been the case, for often policies seem to lurch from a general statement of principles into specifics without any real coherence. Lack of clarity about underlying values that drive policies can lead to a superficial view of what terms like 'inclusion' or for that matter 'a good life' mean. Failure to have an explicit understanding of what underpins these policies can lead to confusion in practice. For example, is it enough to have a house of one's own in the community, a job and relationships to have a good life? How many of these things (if they are relevant) do we need before a life is called good? Just being present in the community does not equate to inclusion. And on whose lives do we base 'an ordinary life' given the diversity of communities and groups in our societies?

Further, an examination of these policies suggests that they often extrapolate from dominant discourses in the wider community to people with intellectual disabilities. Such discourses themselves provide an ill-defined idea of what a good life means in the wider social context. Even between the two authors there are differences in the weight we give to different elements of a good life. What then about the differences between people much more diverse in outlook than the two of us? After all we share gender, age and many common interests. And yet there seem to be some common themes in the values underpinning policies for people with intellectual disabilities. Is there some kind of dominant, though unstated, discourse of a good life in our society that is then applied to this group?

The importance of this question was given added weight by a view we held that historically the lives of people with intellectual disabilities had been formed and shaped sometimes consciously and sometimes unconsciously by contemporary community values, knowledge and power. So, for example, the institutionalisation of many people with intellectual disabilities in the early 20th century could be seen in part as a reflection of wider societal concerns about eugenics, the need to differentiate children in terms of 'intelligence' as a result of compulsory education, the need for a new kind of workforce and the development of the new science of psychology (Rose, 1979; Johnson and Tait, 2003). The segregation that institutionalisation involved also reflected ways in which other minority groups, such as indigenous people or black Americans, were treated at the time (Snyder and Mitchell, 2006). We were interested in how far the current policies of government, and the way people with intellectual disabilities live or are expected to live, reflect wider societal values, concerns and conceptions of a good life in our times.

What meanings have we given to a good life for human beings in Western societies?

Trying to garner the views of philosophers and thinkers about the nature of a good life has proved to be challenging. In part this is because so much has been written about this issue. In fact the discipline of philosophy has been in large part articulated as 'teaching us how to live life well' (Grayling, 2003; 2007; Eagleton, 2007). Such a goal would also be held by some theologians in relation to religion and more recently by some sociologists and psychologists. We are writing from within the disability field looking out. As a historian and a psychologist respectively, we draw on these disciplines throughout this chapter. However it was impossible to explore some of the meanings of a good life without considering some of the themes and issues they raise in philosophy and social thought.

We offer in these pages not a detailed account of a good life, but rather a play across four themes – pleasure/virtue/duty, happiness, reason and freedom – that seem to underpin views of a good life and that we think are of particular relevance to the construction of this by and for people with intellectual disabilities.

A good life: The use of reason and the place of passion

The getting of wisdom

Foolish Jack exchanged a cow for beans to his mother's horror. The beans became a ladder to the sky where Jack through painful experiences with the giant ruler gained sufficient wisdom to gain wealth and a beautiful wife. But the getting of wisdom was not the only motivating force in Jack's story. His concern to raise his mother from her poverty-stricken existence, falling in love with a beautiful woman, captured by the giant and a good dose of greed appear to have been motivating factors as well.

Jack's story is problematic morally. On one reading he is a thieving villain who gains a good life finally by murdering the giant who is seeking to regain his stolen property. On another reading, however, he is the archetypal hero, found in many of our myths and fairy tales. He begins life foolish, takes a journey, which always involves painful experiences, and learns to use wisdom and judgement to gain a good life for himself and others. Such stories usually include a mentor who shares wisdom and from whom the hero gains support, and strong feelings that drive him (it's nearly always a hero!) through his adventures to a happy life … ever after. This raises a number of questions about the place of reason, wisdom and passion in shaping a good life.

From the Greek philosophers to contemporary ethicists the importance of reason in the development of a 'good life' has been a recurrent theme. The centrality of reason in the framing of a good life takes a number of different forms. For example, in an exploration of philosophy and the good life, Cottingham (1998) suggests three different approaches to the place of reason in the good life. In the first, which he labels rational exclusionism, reason is seen as central to a good life, which is defined in narrow intellectual terms. For example, for Plato the good life consisted in the life of a philosopher, dedicated to a search for truth and committed to a journey that would transcend the ephemeral and illusory flickering shadows of everyday life (Plato, 1966) and the dangers of passion and feeling:

> To the Platonic way of thinking the passions were always inherently dangerous, always threatening the health and stability of the individual (and the society). The good life is the life of reason – a life whose ultimate worth depends on the systematic pursuit of rational inquiry. (Cottingham, 1998, p 39)

A second approach to the place of reason in the good life was labelled by Cottingham as rational hegemonism, in which a good life involves the development of 'a full range of human capacities and dispositions' (Cottingham, 1998, p 36), but only under the guidance of reason, which manages and controls our passions and appetites when they are rebellious. For Aristotle, who is seen as an exponent of this perspective, a truly good life is attained when passions and habits are consistent with reason and they live compatibly together. The third position in relation to the centrality of reason in the good life is advanced by Cottingham as rational instrumentalism, in which reason does not lead in the journey towards a good life, but provides the means by which goals set by 'sentiment' can be obtained. Such a view was espoused by David Hume, who argued that our moral principles were not the result of reasoned decision making, but rather a feeling response to a perceived act (Eagleton, 2007). For Hume, fundamental to a good life were what he termed the natural virtues, which included:

> Friendship, faithfulness, generosity, courage, mercy, fairness, patience, good humour, perseverance, prudence and kindness ... and ... the sociable virtues of good-nature, cleanliness, decorum and being agreeable and handsome enough to render a person lovely or loveable. (Grayling, 2003, p148)

It was in the cultivation of these virtues, friendships and sociability that a good life could be lived.

While the centrality of reason in the creation of a good life may have originated with the Greek philosophers, it was also informed by the movement known as the Enlightenment in the 18th century. Enlightenment philosophers held the view that the world and ourselves were capable of being understood by the systematic application of scientific reason, which would enable us to discover the fundamental laws that governed nature and humankind. This entailed an optimistic view of human history in which human progress is related to our increasing knowledge and understanding. The centrality of reason in this development was shaken in the 20th century. Freud's exposition of the unconscious with its implication that we are not creatures of reason and do not exercise it in many of our decisions, and his view that there is a large part of the unconscious that would be forever largely unknown (Freud and Strachey, 2001), cast doubt on the idea of human beings as rational. The negative effects of science as used in major wars and in the environmental degradation accompanying scientific progress have led to a questioning of the capacity of reason to develop a good life for individuals or for humanity at large.

However, while the centrality of reason has been under question it still remains an important underpinning of our views of a good life. The philosopher and ethicist Peter Singer (1993; Singer and Kuhse, 2002) places it centrally as one of the key things that makes us human. Singer is one of the few philosophers to discuss disability, however his view leads to very negative conclusions (see further discussion in Part Three). For example, he argues that without the capacity for conscious experience, reflection, planning or memory a disabled infant:

> will not experience pain or suffering, [but] neither will it experience pleasure or joy – or any of the things that make life valuable. (Singer and Kuhse, 2002, p 237)

In Singer's view reason allows us to step outside our daily immersion in life and to consider for both ourselves and others what a good life might be and to take an active role in its development at a social level.

If the centrality of reason in shaping and defining a good life has engrossed much of philosophical thought in Western societies it raises questions about the place of passion and emotion in our lives. Are they a part of humanity that needs to be tamed, ignored or regarded as 'animal energies' unrelated to reason? It is significant that all philosophers referred to so far are men. Women philosophers and writers have more latterly found a voice in challenging the hegemony of reason and have deconstructed it in gendered terms (Gilligan, 1991) or stressed the importance of emotion and passion in our lives (Murdoch, 1993). Nussbaum (2001b) offers a critique of the centrality of reason arguing that emotions are 'intelligent responses to the perception of value' (Nussbaum, 2001b, p 1). Using a personal example of the complex emotions she experienced at the death of her mother, she argues that emotions are about something or someone. They are not mindless or free-floating. Further they depend on how we see the person or situation and how that relates to our perceptions of ourselves and our own lives. So the grief and fear she felt at her mother's impending death revealed both the value of her mother to her and her fear of loss. Differentiating between different emotions depends on the perception of the situation or individual to whom the emotion is directed. Further, emotions involve a system of complex beliefs about the object, so, for example, fear involves a complex set of beliefs, which includes the belief that something bad is impending and that this is out of the individual's control. These beliefs are integral to the emotions that we feel for otherwise we could not differentiate between them. Finally she argues that emotions are concerned with the value of the object to the individual. Without this investment we would not respond emotionally to it. Consequently, Nussbaum contends that regarding our moral and ethical decisions as driven by intellect alone leaves out an important part of what shapes them. Emotions themselves she argues are 'suffused' with intelligence and discernment and are consequently 'part and parcel of the system of ethical reasoning' (Nussbaum, 2001b, p 1).

While Nussbaum's account of the place of emotion in informing our ethical systems is important there can be little doubt that there is a continuing emphasis within philosophy and social theory on the importance of reason in shaping the good life, whether this is focused on making ethical decisions or in the creation of 'happiness'.

A good life: pleasure/virtue/duty

The choice?

As a young man, so the tales have it, the legendary strong man Hercules was accosted by the personification of Duty and Pleasure in the form of attractive women, each adjuring him to follow her into the life she represented. The story attracted painters, poets and composers of the late Renaissance as emblematic of the crucial juncture all must face in life. One might put it by saying that it represents the dividing of the ways leading respectively to the good life and the Good Life. (Grayling, 2007, p 1)

Hercules chose Duty with its attendant immortal fame rather than the immediacy of Pleasure, in his case described in terms of lifelong ease, unlimited entertainment and sex with the most beautiful of women. The story poses a distinction between a Good Life, which is seen as one of duty and 'virtue', and one that is given to pleasure. Such a division between the two is a continuing theme in both philosophy and religion.

Hercules' 'choice' resurfaced in a different context in Christian belief, with duty seen as a careful preparation in this life for the next. Duty might be its own reward, but in much Christian thought and teaching it was also accompanied by an eternal life of bliss that was available only to those who were loving, mild, meek, chaste, self-sacrificing and obedient to the teaching of the Church(es) (Grayling, 2003). Other than for members of some heavily persecuted sects, like the Cathars in medieval France (Ladurie, 1990), the promise of everlasting life was not there for those rollicking sensualists who trod the broad way to Hell. For both Hercules and those who subscribed to the duty offered through religious belief, the choice is stark: there is no possibility of combining pleasure and duty.

In contrast to the Christian view of virtue, pleasure is focused very much on life in this world rather than being a preparation for the next, either in terms of immortal fame or everlasting life:

> A good life includes pleasure. Surely if there is consensus on anything about living well, it would be on that. We reflect on our lives and plan for our futures and none of us is indifferent to either the joys we have known – they make our memories sweet – or the joys we want our plans and projects to make room for. (Russell, 2005, p 1)

This quotation, which begins a book-long exploration of how Plato placed pleasure in the context of a good life, is significant. First, it asserts that pleasure does have a part in the development of a good life. It is important because it 'helps us to do things and to do them well' (Russell, 2005, p 2), so because we enjoy an activity it leads us to persevere and to become better at it. Pleasure forms part of the basis for friendship as we share 'pleasures' with others and it is a way of discovering others' values and interests. Russell also comments that pleasure changes with age, with differing lifestyles and with changing values and interests. So in Marie's life history, which begins this book, she now finds pleasure in things that before were closed to her: dancing and the pleasures gained from public-speaking and travel. Further pleasure informs our judgements about others in terms of the ways they do or do not indicate pleasure in actions in which we are involved.

Second, the quotation suggests, and Russell's later argument emphasises, that pleasure does not equate with a good life. Russell's statement makes it clear that while pleasure might inform our plans and memories, it remains contingent on how we think about them. So while we may find it difficult to envisage a good life totally without pleasure, it is not sufficient for one. Pleasure is by its nature episodic and transitory. Some forms of pleasure, which Russell defines as sensation, for example the relief of physical discomfort, are particularly fleeting. Others, which he defines as an attitude that is focused on particular objects or events, are less so. So we think back on times that gave us pleasure or we prepare for future pleasures. Or we are currently engaged in an activity that is pleasurable, but which is finite in its duration.

Further, Russell argues that pleasure does depend on other factors, in particular it is strongly related to the underlying values and the direction we give our lives. It is not 'either' good or bad in itself, but only in so far as it reflects the goodness or badness of the person experiencing it. For example, it is clear from this quotation that pleasure is linked to our inner values and the way we reflect on our lives. It is in Plato's terms, a conditional good. That is, it relies on our reflection of our life as a whole and on how we define that which is good for us and others.

For Plato virtue seen as wisdom is the directive force in our lives that is essential for a good life, and which, unlike pleasure, is a non-conditional good. Wisdom shapes our lives and gives positive value to the experiences and pleasures that we own. So, for Plato at least, the good life is dependent on the use of wisdom or virtue and with that will come pleasures that are themselves contingent on the underlying wisdom that guides the person through their life.

A good life: happiness: the never-ending quest?

The pursuit of happiness

There was once a fisherman and his wife who lived together happily by the sea. They had friends, enough to live on as the sea yielded a regular supply of food supplemented with what they grew and traded. They were healthy and in their view they were leading a good life. One day the fisherman caught a large fish that offered him a wish in exchange for freedom. The fisherman consulted his wife who suggested a larger house. It happened. Her desires were not satisfied. Her husband sought the fish again ... and again. The large house become a castle, the pair kings and queens, the castle became home of the Pope where the fisherman and his wife reigned supreme. It was only when the wish was to become God that the fish rebelled and reduced the fisherman and his wife to their original state.

While this salutary fairy story can be read as a condemnation of greed, it can also throw some light on how happiness has been seen as fundamental to a good life. It emphasises the difference between happiness as a state that is continuing, and happiness as an always elusive phenomenon that can never be finally attained. It also construes a view of happiness as an additive one, the more one has, the happier one expects to be. This additive vision of a good life has been neatly summed up by Julian Barnes in relation to the way many middle-class people live in a modern Western society:

> We encourage one another towards the secular modern heaven of self-fulfilment: the development of the personality, the relationships which help define us, the status giving job, the material goods, the ownership of property, the foreign holidays, the acquisition of savings, the accumulation of sexual exploits, the visits to the gym, the consumption of culture. It all adds up to happiness, doesn't it – doesn't it? (Barnes, 2008, p 59)

Barnes does not query that happiness is the endgame for a life. The happiness he ironically outlines is an individualistic one, with its leading statement of 'self-fulfilment' and the 'development of the personality' and its emphasis on the individual's success in accumulating material goods. But his doubts about whether this actually adds up to happiness, or indeed to a good life, resonate strongly with other writers who have argued that a good life is more than the sum of personal development and consumerism.

'What is wrong with happiness?' is the question that opens Zygmunt Bauman's critique of the current way we give meaning to our lives. He argues that:

> We could even say that our modern era started in earnest with the proclamation of the universal human right to happiness, and from the promise to demonstrate its superiority over the forms of life it replaced by rendering that pursuit less cumbersome and arduous, while being more effective. (Bauman, 2008, p 3)

Such happiness was seen as tied firmly to economic growth, which would provide better lives for individuals. However, he argues, research on happiness in affluent countries has revealed that there may be no connection between rising affluence and happiness. Indeed he sees the consequences of a consumerist approach to 'happiness' as leading to what he has termed the miseries of happiness, which include: the marginalisation of groups of people who do not have equal access to goods, a never-ending struggle for legitimacy and one-upmanship through attaining 'magnificence' and excess, unobtainable by the majority who continue to seek them and a situation where even our moral concerns are only voiced and not acted on.

In Bauman's terms we have exchanged a vision of happiness that was constituted by Aristotle as an attainable continuing state predicated on the gaining of certain specified and obtainable goals, for a constant pursuit of happiness that is not defined and which is based on competition, consumerism and the need to see oneself as superior to others (Bauman, 2008). Within what he terms our 'liquid' society the ideas and the goals of happiness are constantly moving and shifting as we strive towards them. For Bauman, happiness is now part of the way in which we are controlled and managed within our societies, and in the individualism that this entails we have lost a sense of duty to each other, and the commitment to the 'work' in all aspects of our lives that will make them worth living.

The effects of a dominant discourse of happiness in competitive capitalist societies that focuses on the individual has been seen as leading to a situation where our involvement with each other and with our communities becomes more tenuous. Our relationships with others are seen in competitive terms and as individuals we become less and less concerned with the 'community' to which we belong, or the greater good. This critique of perceived Western views of happiness is not restricted to Bauman's account. Other writers have explored the consequences of what has been seen as an increasing alienation of the individual from the community arising from a focus on happiness for the self. For example, Lasch (1995) expressed concern at what he saw as an increasing focus on the need for success and the accumulation of goods by the individual and the subsequent gradual narrowing of the definition of community and our commitments to it. Writing from a community perspective, Putnam (2000) described a decline in what he saw as community involvement by individuals in the USA, and Singer (1993) has offered a critique of the prevailing focus on the individual good at the expense of others and the community. The work of some of these writers is explored in more detail in later chapters of this book.

Bauman's view of how we currently constitute happiness resonates with a view of it as additive, where it depends on the good things in one's life, health and wealth, possessions and relationships. There can never be enough of these things to allow us to enjoy a continuing state of 'happiness'. He is concerned that long-term commitment to each other, individually and socially, and the work of love are no longer valued as part of a good life or as happiness.

For some Greek philosophers and writers, happiness could not be the fundamental basis for a good life. Indeed, some argued that it was only possible to describe a life as happy after the person living it was dead. Happiness was something that came and went during a life and one never knew what bad fortune the gods might suddenly visit on you (McMahon, 2006).

As noted in the account given of pleasure and duty, others advanced a perspective of happiness in which it was seen as depending on 'the intelligent direction that all the areas of one's life take together as a whole directed by practical reason and intelligent agency' (Russell, 2005, p 10). Such a view of happiness is concerned with a holistic and reflective approach to life, which depends on the use of reason to shape and bring together the components of a life to make something that is uniquely the individual's own.

Finally, for a lighter touch in relation to the good life and happiness, Eagleton (2007) provides a metaphor for a good life as a jazz group, explaining it in the following terms:

> Take as an image of the good life, a jazz group. A jazz group which is improvising obviously differs from a symphony orchestra, since to a large extent each member is free to express herself as she likes. But she does so with a receptive sensitivity to the self expressive performances of the other musicians. The complex harmony they fashion comes not from playing from a collective score, but from the free musical expression of each member acting as the basis for the free expression of the others.... There is no conflict here between freedom and the 'good of the whole' yet the image is the reverse of totalitarian. (Eagleton, 2007, p 99)

This metaphor, as is always the case, has its limits. But it fits with the views expressed by some of the critics of our current views of happiness or indeed a good life. Eagleton's metaphor suggests the need for a life lived both separately and together, with a commitment to the development of something of worth or beauty through the interplay of the creativity, reflection and considered judgement of the individual in concert with others:

> It is the wish of all men … to live happily,
> But when it comes to seeing clearly what it is that makes life happy,
> They grope for the light;
> Indeed, a measure of the difficulty of achieving the happy life
> Is that the greater the man's energy in striving for it,
> The further he gets away from it
> If he has taken the wrong turning on the road. (Seneca, 1928–35, *On the happy life*)

If happiness remains elusive and difficult to find it was equally difficult to define it in writing about it. The theorists discussed in this section have largely documented what they see as 'the wrong turning on the road' that has made the achievement of happiness difficult. From the perspective of these writers the current views of happiness cannot make it the basis for a good life. Rather this is seen in terms of work, reflection and meaning achieved through the use of judgement and the growth of wisdom in communion with others. Such a view of a good life resonates strongly with a statement attributed to Freud that the meaning of life is work and love.

A good life: freedom and constraint

Freedom and constraint

Lucifer was one of God's most loved angels. In Milton's *Paradise lost*, he leads a failed revolution against God's power and is hurled with his cohorts from Heaven to deepest Hell. Rising from the sea of fire he calls on his comrades to rise and proclaims:

> The mind is its own place, and in itself
> Can make a heaven of hell, a hell of heaven
> What matter where, if I be still the same
> And what I should be, all but less than he
> Whom thunder hath made greater? Here at least

> We shall be free; the almighty hath not built
> Here for his envy, will not drive us hence:
> Here we may reign secure, and in my choice
> To reign is worth ambition though in hell:
> Better to reign in hell, than serve in heaven. (Milton, 2005, pp 24–5)

Pullman, in his introduction to *Paradise lost* comments that his sympathies lie with Lucifer and this has been a common response to Milton's account of his fall from grace. Perhaps, in part, our sympathies lie with Lucifer because of his assertion of individuality, choice and freedom from the constraints involved in obedience to God's will, for freedom and the individual have been important factors shaping the way we now see a good life in Western societies. However, Lucifer's transformation from angel of light to the king of darkness also stands as a dire warning about the consequences of lack of constraint and the need for some kind of obedience if we are to live in company with others. There is a tension between the appetites and the consequences of unrestrained freedom and the need to protect the others with whom we live.

It is probably clear from the earlier parts of this chapter that for many philosophers the attainment of a good life (however construed) is seen to come from within the individual, through the exercise of reason, combined with 'good values' and with passions and emotions holding variable positions. There seems to us to be a premise here that individuals exercise choices in relation to their own life although at different times the constraints on such choices will differ depending on the status and position of the individual or the broader social and political context in which they live. Such a view is predicated on the perceived capacity of people to make 'good choices'.

If people are not seen as being able to make such choices, then the need for constraint becomes necessary. Philosophers have advanced the position that human beings by their nature cannot be allowed a totally free choice but that, in order to gain some measure of fairness or justice, constraints on individual freedom must be made. These ideas have found their clearest expression in ideas of a social contract. So Hobbes argues that the essential equality between human beings leads inevitably to a state of war if they are unrestrained because they are in competition for the goods of the world, because they fear the loss of what they have and because they seek glory over others. Such a state of war leads to 'the life of man, solitary, poor, nasty, brutish and short' (Hobbes, 1969, p 143). For Hobbes, the only way that peace and some degree of fairness can be obtained when people live together is for them to form a contract by which they renounce their 'right' to act and their liberty to do so without constraint and transfer power to one person or to a group to govern them in order to attain peace and common defence.

The social contract envisaged by Hobbes is an individualistic one that seeks to provide maximum freedom combined with personal security for each person subject to it (Vardy and Grosch,1999). The idea of a social contract advanced by Hobbes has been developed and framed differently by later philosophers and thinkers (see, for example, Locke, Haslett, 1988; Rousseau, 1996).

It is beyond the remit of this chapter to explore the different ways in which social contracts have been conceptualised by philosophers over the last several hundred years, however the ideas of John Rawls have particular significance for the issues in this book. Rawls (1999) argues from what he terms an original position where people come together in order to lay the foundations for a just society in the form of a social contract, which is defined as 'a hypothetical agreement in an original position of equality. Rawls invites us to ask what principles we – as rational, self-interested persons would choose if we found ourselves in that position' (Sandel, 2009, p 141). Both self-interest and a veil of ignorance behind which we do not know what our actual position will be in society are important in his view of a social contract. We are unlikely to choose principles that might disadvantage us if we in reality find ourselves disadvantaged. The other assumptions on which Rawls' development of a social contract are based are that people are equal to one another in their ability and freedom to make suggestions about how society should be organized, all have knowledge of human and social affairs, and people are rational and able to participate in the development of a social contract (Vardy and Grosch, 1999).

In this situation Rawls argues that we will as rational human beings develop a contract that rests on two principles:

- A principle of liberty: people must be allowed the freedom to pursue the kind of life they would wish to lead provided it does not directly or indirectly harm another. This principle provides equal basic liberties for all citizens. It is given high priority by Rawls in his theory (Sen, 2009).
- The second principle is concerned with economic and social equality. It does not require an equal distribution of income and wealth. However it only allows such inequalities if they work to improve the situation of those who are most disadvantaged.

The operation of these principles in the institutions of society is seen by Rawls as providing a basis for a society in which justice as fairness may operate.

Individual freedom is important in Rawls' conception of a social contract and so is the maintenance of choice and difference. Further he accepts that inequality is inevitable, however to maintain the contract decisions will be made that must favour the least well-off.

Rawls has had an immense influence on social theory and philosophy. However, as Nussbaum (2006) comments, his theory excludes from the social contract those whose 'reason' is not seen as equal. This raises particular issues for people labeled as having intellectual disabilities since they are not seen as equal participants in the formulation of a just and fair society.

Freedom and the choices we make as individuals have been strong and repeated themes underlying ideas of a good life. Yet as we have seen in this section philosophers have also struggled with how such freedom can be protected and how the interests of all can be taken into account. It would seem that some kind of constraint needs to be imposed on the fulfilment of desires by the individual if the good of the many is to be safeguarded.

Conclusion

Humanity seems to be on a never-ending journey in which a good life remains a sought-after but elusive goal. There are, however, some points that can be drawn from our account. The good life in Western thought has been very focused on the individual: on their values and on the way in which choices made in life are related to these. It also has a strong and continuing emphasis on the place of reason and reflection in shaping one's life. And yet there is also a recognition of the need for constraints if people are to live together safely and in harmony. Underpinning this view are concepts of justice that will be developed later in this book.

We have also found that there is a need to explore the meaning of terms that we use as if we all understood their meaning (for example 'a good life') or where there are real differences between them that are often unacknowledged (for example pleasure and happiness). Further while it may not be possible to define a good life it is possible to identify some things that may prevent it from occurring. Oppression, lack of safety, a failure to recognise the rights of others, a narrow imposed definition of an assumed good such as happiness, and a failure to consider how passion and reason might work together within one person's life are some of the issues that we acknowledge.

We have not in this discussion considered the issue of what a life is. And yet this is important in thinking about 'a good life'. The term itself suggests something unitary and certainly when we reflect on our lives we see them as a continuous stream. However, both Bauman (2008) and Giddens (1991) assert strongly that modern life at least is 'episodic', a series of narratives, an art that we create, which changes over time and as our goals, desires and needs alter. Such a view makes the idea of a 'good life' even for one individual ever more difficult to define.

Marie's life story suggests that for her a good life is framed around having a home, a job and relationships. However our reading of a good life suggests that there are very different views of what a good life means. It is possible to reinterpret her desires and dreams in terms of a strongly individualistic approach that stresses autonomy and independence. And an important part of her life is the need to support and promote a better life for those whom she sees as less well-off. Yet many of the things that frame her view of a good life are not the things that have been persistent themes in philosophical discussions. Indeed, for example, the pursuit of happiness or pleasure has been criticised as the basis for a good life.

Where does this discussion leave us in terms of considering a good life and people with intellectual disabilities? The following chapter explores some of these issues.

THREE

A good life and people with intellectual disabilities

Philosophical and social-theoretical accounts of what makes a good life seem far from the lived experience of people with intellectual disabilities. However, in this chapter we reflect on the implications of such theories and ideas for how a good life is framed and understood in the context of the lives of people with intellectual disabilities. In undertaking this task we explore the second of the questions that provide the framework for this book: what are the implications for people with intellectual disabilities of thinking about the good life?

From the account in Chapter Two of some of the themes that have been seen to constitute a good life we identified a series of sub-questions that seem to be related to the broad question posed above. These are:

- Given the strong focus on the importance of reason in philosophical thought on a good life, what are the consequences for groups of people whose reason is perceived as flawed, impaired or 'inferior' to those around them?
- Does this preclude them from leading a 'good life'?
- If, as it would seem, a good life is integrally related to the inner life of the individual, how do we find out what people with intellectual disabilities want?
- What emphasis, if any, should be given to 'duty', 'virtue' and commitment to others in the lives of people with intellectual disabilities?
- If people are unable to show us that they are 'reflective' or 'plan for the future' how do we then consider a good life for and by them?
- How have the tensions between the freedom of the individual and constraint been played out in the way a good life is conceived for people with intellectual disabilities?
- If we accept the critique of modern happiness offered by Bauman, what does this mean for a good life for people with intellectual disabilities?
- Are people with intellectual disabilities restricted to a life of 'pleasure', planned for them and given value by others?

Each section of this chapter deals with a subset of these questions.

Reason

What are the implications of a good life that is focused on reason for people with intellectual disabilities? Given the strong focus on the importance of reason in philosophical thought about a good life, what are the consequences for groups of people whose reason is perceived as flawed, impaired or 'inferior' to those around them? Does this preclude them from leading a 'good life'?

> "I never want to be like that. Never. I'd rather be dead, I don't want that life. It's just not for me. You just feel you're nobody, no life, you're not recognised. People will do everything for you. It's not me so I always worry. I always have that on my mind, you know. If my memory got worse I'd have to go back, there's nothing anybody could do. I'd just go back, you know, if I deteriorate you know, if I got cancer, if my memory did start going I'd have to go back you know, I just don't want to."

A woman thinking about her life. Afraid. Feeling anxious that she will lose what little power she currently has. Reflecting. And a woman with an intellectual disability. Marie's fears and anxieties are premised on views about what a good life should be: one in which she has independence, opportunities for fulfilment, for meaning and close relationships. Throughout her life history she talks of the values that underpin her life. Marie makes it clear that gaining acknowledgement by others for these ideas, for the trajectory of her life, has been, and remains, difficult. Her fear of lack of recognition as a person encapsulates some of the arguments presented in Chapter Two of this part of the book. When reason is impugned a person is not recognised, that person may not be even seen as fully human and may not be seen as being able to develop the individually formed and defined good life. It may then be created for them by others.

The centrality of the ability to use reason has been stressed by many philosophers writing about a good life. When reason is impugned people may find themselves excluded not only from a good life, but also from any consideration by others that they are able to reflect or to develop an internal life of values, beliefs, hopes and dreams. As noted in Chapter Two, their very status as human beings may be doubted.

People with intellectual disabilities live with labels that carry an integral message of flawed or impugned reason: mental retardation, mental handicap, intellectual disability, learning disability, all carry with them the message that this person may have difficulties (of varying kinds) in exercising a capacity for reason and abstract thought. So, the American Association of Mental Retardation (AAMR, 2002) defined 'mental retardation' in the following terms:

> Mental retardation is a disability characterized by significant limitations both in intellectual functioning and in adaptive behavior as expressed in conceptual, social and practical adaptive skills. This disability originates before age 18.
>
> The following five assumptions are essential to the application of this definition:
>
> 1. Limitations in present functioning must be considered within the context of community environments typical of the individual's age peers and culture.
> 2. Valid assessment considers cultural and linguistic diversity as well as differences in communication, sensory, motor, and behavioral factors.
> 3. Within an individual, limitations often coexist with strengths.
> 4. An important purpose of describing limitations is to develop a profile of needed supports.
> 5. With appropriate personalized supports over a sustained period, the life functioning of the person with mental retardation generally will improve.
> (AAMR, 2002, p 1)

This definition (in spite of the assumptions accompanying it) reveals the way in which impaired reason is attributed to people with intellectual disabilities. They are defined as a single group whose members have fundamentally flawed reason and whose life functioning may only improve with personalised support over a long period of time.

As discussed in the previous chapter, reason is central to the good life in Western philosophy. This is revealed in a number of different ways:

- The use of reason is equated with the good life by some philosophers and for others it is a necessary component.
- Reason enables the control of perceived destructive passions and desires.
- For some philosophers the capacity to reason is what largely defines us as human beings.
- Only those with 'reason' are seen as able to enter into the fundamental social contract by which we live together in harmony and to varying degrees in justice.

If reason is accepted as central to the way we conceive a good life, then it is apparent that for people with intellectual disabilities this will not be perceived as attainable because they are seen as people whose reason is flawed. The way in which most Western philosophers have construed the importance of reason also detracts from people's standing as 'human beings' and perhaps helps us to understand the power of earlier discourses that constituted them as dangerous and a threat to society (Tredgold, 1952; Johnson, 1998; Jackson 2001).

In the Introduction to this book, Table 1 showed people with intellectual disabilities as marginalised and often unable to access services and ways of life that the rest of the population take for granted. The continuing philosophical focus on the importance of reason in defining us as persons and in creating a good life marginalises people not only socially and economically, but also as human beings.

Of course not everyone reads philosophy, yet the focus on reason and on intellectual functioning is deeply engrained in the way we see ourselves, each other and our society and has shaped the lives of people with intellectual disabilities through, for example, the use of IQ tests and eugenics. So IQ tests were designed to identify people with 'flawed reason' and impaired intellectual functioning with the aim of ensuring that they could be 'managed' in a way that would protect both them from society and society from them (Rose, 1979; Johnson and Tait, 2003).

As discussed in the previous chapter, many Western philosophers have advanced the view that the really authentic good life arises from within, from reflection, and from values that lead to wisdom. The failure to acknowledge an inner life for people with intellectual disabilities (Sinason, 1992; Johnson, 1998), which in part stems from the importance we give to reason, can mean that the possibility of creating such a life is denied. In the absence of a perceived autonomous, fully reasoning individual a good life is created around the person by others. When this happens inevitably the most positive focus can become the creation of pleasure and happiness symbolised in 20th-century society by material possessions, independence and autonomy. This involves a projection of wider societal values of the time onto people with intellectual disabilities. For Marie these things are important, but her story is particularly powerful because of her insight that these things created around her and for her are not enough. She comments:

> "People probably think 'oh you've got a job, that's fine' but that isn't what I want, really you know. I think it's time to do something different, completely different, you know."

For people with intellectual disabilities it is enough, in the eyes of others, to have a paid job, the semblance of meaning. The fact that Marie finds the work unsatisfying is of little importance to those around her.

The view that people with intellectual disabilities have impaired reason may thus stop us from hearing what they do want or supporting them to find out. Rather, their supporters, workers and families seek, at best, to provide a life that can be called 'good' in terms of the goods and issues that can be arranged externally.

This is exacerbated by the all-encompassing label of intellectual disability or learning disability, which identifies widely diverse individuals as one group. The failure to consider the differences within this group means that there is a 'one-stop-shop' view of a good life that is seen as equally applicable to all. Yet Marie's life and her wishes, desires and concerns are unique to her and are based on her ability to lead a largely independent life. For others with intellectual disabilities this is not the case. For some people, the use of spoken language is difficult or impossible, while others require high levels of support to survive physically in the world. There is, in our view, a need to think more carefully about the differences that exist within the group labelled as having intellectual disabilities and to consider what a good life might mean for them, not as a group, but much more on an individual basis. For some people with high support needs or with little or no spoken language the values underpinning the Western concept of a good life may need to be revisited. A focus on reason, virtue and freedom may need to be revised, and our need as human beings for interdependence or an unpacking of what dependence may mean in people's lives could be considered. The use of supported decision making can be helpful in these circumstances, however if this occurs only within the existing value framework we believe that it may devalue other ways of leading a good life. The important issue for us in considering the diversity of people who wear the label intellectual disabilities is that those working with them do so from a values base that does not exclude frameworks that may lie outside of the dominant Western discourse of a good life.

The 20th century saw the rise of the social sciences, particularly psychology, which has focused on efforts to increasingly understand the nature of persons and groups. In the process of this development there was a focus on identifying and measuring constructs such as 'intelligence'. We are not sure that intelligence and reason are the same, but they are conflated in accounts of people with intellectual disabilities as in the definition offered by the AAMR. Intelligence itself was seen as a global construct, but is now seen by some theorists as differentiated into different forms of intelligence (Gardner, 1990). Yet this view does not seem to have been taken up strongly when applied to people with intellectual disabilities. The idea promulgated by Martha Nussbaum that the emotions and passions are a form of intelligence or reason that should be recognised is not one that occurs in the literature about people with intellectual disabilities. A notable exception to this way of thinking is Sinason's (1992) argument that an intellectual disability does not necessarily mean that someone lacks emotional intelligence.

Pleasure, duty and virtue

What emphasis if any should be given to 'duty', 'virtue' and commitment to others in the lives of people with intellectual disabilities? What is the role of pleasure in the lives of people with intellectual disabilities?

> "My dream is to keep going and help people as much as I can, that's all I want to do, and keep being here in my flat, that's my dream."
>
> "[I was chairperson of the National Council.] I resigned. I think I wanted to take a break. Then I came back. I was really committed to it. I could have taken a full time job a couple of years ago but I didn't do it. I stayed committed to [the Council], and I stayed going to the meetings and everything even though I could have done more with my life. I could have, but I stayed with them you know."

Working to support the rights of others and to contribute to finding ways for them to lead good lives is central to the way Marie sees her life. And it entails sacrifice. The possibility of a job was at least postponed, if not lost, in order to meet a commitment of representing people with intellectual disabilities on the National Council. In the light of Marie's comments and the discussion in the previous chapter, it seems odd now that, when we began this book, the idea of a good life for people with intellectual disabilities as one that included virtue or duty as central themes was not in the forefront of our thoughts at all.

Our lack of emphasis on the strong theme of virtue in ideas about a good life may reflect 21st-century values that have shifted away from a traditional philosophical or religious base for it, or they may reflect the ways in which people with intellectual disabilities are currently seen by those around them. In policies and planning for people with intellectual disabilities (as we shall see later) a life of virtue or duty is not one that seems to have a strong focus. Indeed, in areas of life that are seen to involve issues of duty or care for others, people with intellectual disabilities have found it difficult to find a recognised place. So, for example, becoming a parent and forming intimate adult relationships remain areas that are very problematic (Walmsley 1993; Booth and Booth, 1994; Shakespeare et al, 1996; Johnson et al, 2001). Further, although making a contribution to the lives of others is listed among the accomplishments deemed important to consider in planning for people with intellectual disabilities (O'Brien and Lyle, 1987), in practice it often seems as if issues of adult responsibilities are omitted from a consideration of people's lives − or not acknowledged. This happens in spite of the sizeable contribution many people with intellectual disabilities make: in work as carers for older parents or relatives (Walmsley, 1993), in labour as unpaid helpers in institutions (Rolph 2000, Reaume 2006), and the unpaid contribution many make through work in self-advocacy organisations or by volunteering (see, for example, Millear with Johnson, 2000; Slattery with Johnson, 2000). There are numerous instances where there is reciprocity, where, like Marie, the altruism associated with a gift relationship is demonstrated (Titmuss, 1961, 1971). Yet it is rarely recognised as such, or acknowledged, but rather cast in terms such as work preparation, time filling or therapy.

The seeming difficulty in acknowledging the possible place of duty and virtue and care for others in the lives of people with intellectual disabilities stems from a view of them as not being able to exercise the reflection and empathy needed to undertake such tasks. Rather, people with this label are seen as subject to the care and duty of others. This view framed early 20th-century policies that identified people with intellectual disabilities within a medical discourse and institutionalised many of them, ostensibly for their own care and protection, but also to remove them as a potentially dangerous burden on others in society (see Chapter Five). Not all people with intellectual disabilities can make decisions about duty and virtue (which is also true of many people without intellectual disabilities!). Not all can contribute in practical ways. Our argument here is not that people should be urged to undertake such roles, but rather that they should be seen as a possible theme or ingredient in any good life.

Virtue and duty in relation to the lives of people with intellectual disabilities are more likely to be seen in relation to those who work with them or who are family members. They are subject to the exercise of duty and virtue in the lives of others. So feminist research into caring in the 1980s (Abbot and Sapsford, 1997; Dalley, 1988) focused on the difficulties confronting mothers with a child with disabilities and research and literature in the disability field continues to focus on the stresses and strains of family life in caring for a disabled family member (Walmsley and Mannan, 2009).

For Hercules the choice between pleasure and virtue was stark. For many of us over a lifetime pleasure and duty are intertwined. Without expectations that a person will be involved in developing a life that includes and indeed is based on the acquisition of virtue, the issue of transitory pleasures, though strictly boundaried when it comes to sensual ones, can become the focus of consideration for those working with people with intellectual disabilities. As Cottingham (1998) comments (see Chapter Two), pleasure is strongly related to the values that we hold and demands some recognition of an interior life. Without the attribution of such values the idea of pleasure becomes one that is projected onto the person with intellectual disabilities by those around them. Even when a person indicates what gives them pleasure either through spoken language or non-verbally, such pleasures are subject to the approval of others and their values. It is also difficult in the light of the previous discussion of pleasure to see this as a strong element in the development of a good life. It is an accompaniment certainly, but not the key focus.

Happiness

If we accept the critique of modern happiness offered by Bauman, what does this mean for a good life for people with intellectual disabilities?

> "I like shopping, looking at things, like. I like clothes, wearing clothes. I thought one time I'd like to be a model but I think it's too hard work. I think you have to be a lot

thinner for a model, but I don't think that's me really. I'm
kind of a people person."

It is perhaps significant in the light of Bauman's analysis of happiness
in our society that while Marie says she enjoys shopping, she also
comments that she likes 'looking at things'. Bauman's view of our
pursuit of happiness is very much focused on a never-ending search
for possessions and for status. Both of these are difficult for people
with intellectual disabilities for whom poverty is often a permanent
accompaniment to their lives (Emerson et al, 2005). Bauman offers a
critical view of happiness as a goal for a good life in modern society.
He makes the point that the pursuit of happiness is a never-ending one,
where the goals keep shifting. In our kind of society such happiness
is grounded in material possessions, which inevitably sets us up in
competition with each other. He postulates an additive idea of happiness
that can never be finally attained. Happiness, in Bauman's terms does
not equate with a good life, but rather runs counter to it. Wealth and
privilege are necessary to even engaging in the pursuit.

Yet often in work with people with intellectual disabilities the refrain
is one of creating a situation where people can be happy. Sometimes
this is explicitly stated as an alternative to a full adult life. One parent
in a workshop on sexuality commented that her daughter would
never have adult relationships and that: "I just want her to be happy."
Because this is often a statement from supporters or family members
the happiness is designed for people rather than with them and is
focused on concrete objects. The goals of much government policy
are designed to equate with a modern view of happiness: a house of
one's own, a job and the capacity to acquire possessions are seen as key
issues (see, for example, DH, 2009). If we do not know what individuals
actually see as a good life, then falling back on these things makes sense.
After all they are the goals that many of the rest of us pursue. We are
not arguing here that people should not have a home of their own or
possessions, but are rather suggesting that we need to look at the less
concrete aspects of life as well. In the Introduction, Kelley reflected
on the lives of men who lived in a comfortable house, with support.
She questioned whether this was a good life because of the failure to
explore some of the other aspects of their lives. A home in which one
is alone, or where one's wishes are not considered, or where one is a
virtual prisoner because of lack of resources or support to engage with
others, may not lead to a good life or for that matter to happiness. On
the surface Marie's life fulfils many of the criteria held for a happy life
for people with intellectual disabilities. She has a home of her own,

has had a job and a social life. However throughout her life story there is a yearning for something else, for something not always articulated. Something she feels is missing.

Perhaps one of the lessons from our reading and discussion is that happiness should not be turned into a final goal for a good life. Happiness is something that may come with fulfilment, with comfort and with relationships. It is impossible to legislate for it and not possible to prescribe it. It can accompany a good life, but does not equate with it.

Freedom and constraint

How have the tensions between the freedom of the individual and constraint been played out in the way a good life is conceived for people with intellectual disabilities?

> "In the group homes people never got opportunities to express their feelings or thoughts. You see, some of them in the group homes don't get a chance. It's like they are under 24-hour watch!"

While most Western philosophers have argued strongly for an individualistic view of a good life and one that entails choice directed by reason, some have also argued for the need for constraint, without which, they argue, our lives would be 'nasty brutish and short'. This Hobbesian view of human nature can be seen in some of the discourses that have constituted the lives of people with intellectual disabilities. The view that, having been seen as lacking reason, they will be uncontrolled in their passions and dangerous to themselves and the community was one of the assumptions underlying institutionalisation (Jackson, 2001). While the discourses have changed and people with intellectual disabilities are now more likely to live in the wider community, many of the constraints remain. So, in her life history, Marie focuses in a number of different contexts on the continuing 'gaze' of staff and families to which people with intellectual disabilities are subject. It is clear from her comment at the beginning of this section that such surveillance is not always in terms of 'support', but is also designed to control or to restrain. For at least some people with intellectual disabilities the walls of institutions have been replaced, more latterly, with walls of people whose role is, in part, to gate-keep and mediate the relationships that people with intellectual disabilities establish with other members of society. This is not to argue that such constraint may not be necessary for some people with intellectual disabilities, as it is for other non-disabled citizens. Rather a consideration of the individual and their characteristics and lifestyle should guide the freedom and constraint that they experience and not the presence or absence of a particular label.

There is however a more fundamental concern in a consideration of issues of freedom and constraint in terms of a social contract that provides:

> a general image of society as a contract for mutual advantage (people getting something by living together that they could not get each on their own) among people who are 'free, equal and independent'. (Nussbaum, 2006, p 14)

The social contract is seen as fundamental to the ways in which we govern ourselves, and underpins our views of social justice for those who are seen to be 'signatories'. Nussbaum argues that people with disabilities (as were women and 'slaves' in the past) have been excluded from being seen as participating in the development of a social contract and consequently from participating in political choice. For some people with intellectual disabilities (though not those with severe impairments) this exclusion is, in her view, socially constructed. This exclusion operates in the most recently formulated version of the social contract (Rawls, 1999). For Nussbaum the importance of this relates to the issue of social justice. The social contract is designed and promulgated *by* participants and operates *for* them. Consequently if one is excluded from participation, then one is not considered centrally in the principles of justice that govern the society. She writes:

> Today, when the issue of justice for people with disabilities is prominent on the agenda of every decent society, the omission of all of them from participation in the situation of basic political choice looks problematic, given the evident capacity of many if not most of them for choice; and their omission from the group of persons *for whom* society's most basic principles are chosen is more problematic still. Even if their interests can be taken into account derivatively or at a later stage, we naturally wonder why this postponement is necessary and whether it is not likely to affect the full equal treatment of such citizens – even if it is not in and of itself a form of unequal treatment. (Nussbaum, 2006, p 18)

The failure to include people with intellectual disabilities as fully participating in the way in which our society is structured leads to a marginalisation of citizenship and of justice.

This discussion suggests that for all of us there is a continual tension between freedom and constraint. But for people with intellectual disabilities this operates, as in earlier parts of this chapter, externally rather than internally. They are subject to the gaze and the actions of others in relation to their lives individually and are excluded from fundamental discussions of justice and of the principles that underlie the social contract.

Conclusion

This chapter has offered a reflection on the implications of traditional philosophical views of a good life for people with intellectual disabilities. It has sought to demonstrate that conceptions of this are not only abstractions but also have practical consequences in the lives of people with intellectual disabilities. The chapter has reflected on some of the themes that emerge from traditional views of a good life. It has not sought to suggest alternative views. This will be taken up in Part Three of the book. Part Two is concerned to look in policy and practice terms at how a good life has been conceived for people with intellectual disabilities.

Part Two
Re-examining key concepts in the light of current practice

This part of the book addresses the following questions:

• What values relevant to defining a good life underpin current disability theories, ideas and discourses?
• What contribution have they made to the lives of people with intellectual disabilities?
• How well have the theories been translated into practice by those who work with people with disabilities?

It seeks to deconstruct some of the conceptual and theoretical perspectives that have framed changes and reforms in the lives of people with intellectual disabilities. Its key argument is that the dominant theoretical frameworks of the late 20th century, which have been developed and applied to practice in this field, have not systematically addressed the idea of a good life for people with intellectual disabilities, although some of the themes that we have described earlier in this book seem to be included as part of the theories and policies that have been developed. In particular, the chapter considers the values that underlie each of these conceptualisations and their links to ideas of what makes a good life.

FOUR

A good life in policy

This chapter uses policy developments, the ideas of campaigning theorists and the words of self-advocates themselves in the UK to provide a case study (which is broadly applicable to many other countries in Western Europe, Australasia, the USA and Canada) of changes that have sought to provide a 'better' life for people with intellectual disabilities. We argue that the term 'good life' is rarely used in these contexts. Rather policy makers either use undefined mantras such as 'an ordinary life' or a 'life like any other', or tightly defined terms such as normalisation, social role valorisation or the social model of disability. These ways of thinking and writing and then putting these ideas into practice have led to some positive changes for people with intellectual disabilities. However, in our view they have also camouflaged some of the very real issues that people face in their lives. The chapter identifies continuities in the way life for people with intellectual disabilities has been articulated over three decades. It asks why, given such consistency in aspiration, both over time and between key stakeholders, relatively little progress has been made in people's lives on the ground. Is failure about an implementation gap, as is the common assumption (see, for example, DH, 2009), or does the vision itself need to be questioned? The chapter draws largely on policies developed in England although many of the issues that are raised are also relevant to other Western countries (see Welshman and Walmsley, 2006). We argue that in spite of many changes, the evidence suggests that a good life for most people with intellectual disabilities is still on the far horizon.

This chapter addresses the following questions:

- What values underpin current theories, ideas and discourses?
- What contribution have they made to people's lives?

Ideas about a better life: early stirrings

As noted in the Introduction to this book, few policies actually promulgate explicitly a 'good life' for people with intellectual disabilities. However, ideas about a better life for people with intellectual disabilities began to emerge as a policy goal in the late 1970s. It was then for the first time that it was stated in a British government-commissioned report:

- Mentally handicapped people have a right to enjoy normal patterns of life within the community
- Mentally handicapped people have the right to be treated as individuals
- Mentally handicapped people will require additional help from the communities in which they live and from professional services if they are to develop their maximum potential as individuals.
  (Jay, 1979, p 35)

The vision was fleshed out in an important King's Fund publication, *An ordinary life* (1980), which stated:

Our goal is to see mentally handicapped people in the mainstream of life, living in ordinary houses in ordinary streets, with the same range of choices as any citizen, and mixing as equals with the other, and mostly not handicapped, members of their own community. (p 61)

The thinking was developed by Linda Ward (1995) in her evaluation of the Wells Road housing scheme, which sought to put the 'ordinary life' vision into practice in a working-class area of Bristol. She describes its purpose as follows:

the opportunity to live in a small home, ideally with a companion or companions of one's choice, in an acceptable neighbourhood, with the support that is needed to live an ordinary domestic life and make use of the facilities available nearby. (Ward, 1995, p 5)

Whether an 'ordinary life' is a good life is a moot point. It is, however, interesting to note its key features:

- Own a 'small' home in a local 'acceptable' neighbourhood.
- A choice of whom one lives with.
- Support.
- An 'ordinary domestic life'.

- Use of local, not specialist, services.
- Included in 'local communities'.

Unpicking this neat vision one is struck by its specificity and romanticism. It conjures in the mind an idealised, albeit modest, picture of respectable urban, not rural, life, because nearby facilities are required. It splits the beneficiaries off from other less-privileged groups who, one presumes, live in neighbourhoods that are not 'acceptable'. It presupposes such a thing as an 'ordinary domestic life', without any clarity about whose 'ordinary' this is. This is not, one presumes, the 'ordinary life' of drug-takers, city bankers or world travellers. It is, possibly, the 'ordinary life' of the respectable working class. The idea that there is such a thing as a 'local community' to accept and embrace people is also characteristic of this vision. Further, the term 'ordinary life' itself raises questions. An ordinary life is something that we generally prescribe for others, not something that ideally we would want for ourselves. It emphasises the lack of ordinariness of the lives of people with intellectual disabilities and suggests that while seeking to 'include' them we should also differentiate them from others who may see their lives as far from ordinary.

It would not be accurate to say that this version of an ordinary life immediately became adopted as 'official' government policy. However, it can be demonstrated that elements were incorporated into policy from the early 1980s – the *All Wales strategy* (Welsh Office, 1983), for example, echoed the Jay Report's principles, word for word (Welsh Office, 1983, quoted in Felce et al, 1996, p xii).

Components of this 'ordinary life' have remained fairly constant, although emphases have changed in line, or so we argue, with accompanying changes in the wider society. Constant elements have been:

- The assertion that it is a *right* to have access to normal patterns of life, an ordinary life, a full life, a life like any other.
- Services that are 'person-centred' or more recently 'personalised'.
- Inclusion in 'communities'.
- Access to paid work or meaningful daytime occupation.
- Access to the facilities everyone uses.
- A place of one's own with choices about with whom one lives.

Here is the 2007 English iteration of an ordinary life or, as the minister has it, 'a life like any other':

> There is no question that it is a human rights issue that all people with intellectual disabilities have the choice and control over their lives that so many of us take for granted – a life like any other. (DH, 2007b, p 1)

Valuing people now, which was a revisiting in 2007/08 of the landmark England White Paper, *Valuing people* (DH, 2001), set the following priorities for people with intellectual disabilities:

- Personalisation – real choices over lives and services.
- What people do during the day – with an emphasis on inclusion in communities and access to paid work.
- Access to housing – with a particular emphasis on home ownership and tenancies.
- Making sure change happens (DH, 2009).

Over the years there have indeed been variations on the theme – the 1979 Jay Report's 'right to be treated as individuals' has become 'personalised services'. The aspiration has moved from a small home in the *An ordinary life* publication (King's Fund, 1980), to home ownership. 'Better health' has appeared as a specific objective, rather than an element of access to the services everyone uses, largely because, although this is in place in theory, by and large the outcomes have been, to say the least, disappointing (Clarke and Griffiths, 2008; Michaels, 2008). However, despite minor variations we contend that there has been a remarkable consistency over 30 years in the goals of policies. The need to restate them, albeit in different words, leads to the somewhat depressing conclusion that less progress in creating better lives for people with intellectual disabilities has been made than might have been hoped. *Valuing people now* acknowledges this disappointing lack of progress (DH, 2007b, 2009). In the eyes of the government, it is services that have failed to deliver:

> We can no longer tolerate services which leave people isolated and marginalized. Good quality public services should offer new opportunities for people with intellectual disabilities to lead full and productive lives as valued members of their local communities. (DH, 2007b, p 22)

Note here the repeated rhetoric of 'productive', 'isolated', 'marginalised', 'valued'. None of these terms is defined. These are individualised issues, but combating them is seen as the responsibility of services. Services are expected to deliver more than mere existence, they must combat apathy or hostility by enabling people to be 'valued'; they must conjure up 'communities' where none may exist; they must enable 'full and productive lives'. It is a tall order. This points to a contradiction at the heart of the ideology. It is an individual 'right' to have a 'life like any other', but it is the responsibility of publicly (under)funded services to provide it.

The concept of a normal life

The contribution of normalisation/social role valorisation and the social model of disability

The ideas of campaigning theorists have informed much of the policy development in the past 30 years. It is perhaps not surprising, therefore, that there is little in their ideas that explicitly addresses the idea of a good life. Rather they have focused on ideas of normalising both people with intellectual disabilities, the environments in which they live and the removal of barriers to a 'normal life'. Here we discuss three of the most important sets of ideas that have informed government policy and practice: normalisation, social role valorisation and the social model of disability.

Current policies represent a victory for these ideas. Indeed, so influential have they been across the English-speaking world that it has become almost unthinkable to suggest there may be other ways of approaching the question of how best to support people with intellectual disabilities.

Normalisation

Bank-Mikkelson (1980) in Denmark is credited with being the first to develop the original ideas underpinning normalisation. The idea did not emerge from a vacuum, as we show in Chapter Five. Research had already begun that laid the foundations for reviewing the construction of the 'handicapped' identity. Thus it is but a small step from the arguments put forward by O'Connor and Tizard (1956), that with support and a reasonable environment many people with intellectual disabilities could undertake productive work, to Bank-Mikkelson's proposition that the aim should be:

> an existence for the mentally retarded as close to normal living conditions as possible ... making normal, mentally

retarded people's housing, education, working and leisure conditions. (Bank-Mikkelson, 1980, p 56)

This theme was elaborated by Bengt Nirje who began to talk of normal patterns of living, in which people live, work and enjoy leisure in different places, as happens in 'ordinary life' (Nirje, 1989). Brown and Smith observed presciently in 1992 that this entailed 'ensuring equality on a number of traditional social indicators of quality of life including housing, education, work and leisure' (1992, p 3). As social norms have changed, so have the parameters of normalisation. For instance, in 1980 Nirje specified the right to the development of heterosexual relationships, including the right to marry (quoted in Brown and Smith, 1992, p 2). In the early 21st century this would extend to same-sex relationships, including the right to a civil partnership (DH, 2009).

Social role valorisation

Wolf Wolfensberger, a US-based academic/campaigner, took normalisation ideas further, refashioning them as 'social role valorisation' (SRV). SRV argued for:

> The utilisation of means which are as culturally normative as possible, in order to establish and /or maintain personal behaviors and characteristics which are as culturally normative as possible. (Wolfensberger et al, 1972, p 28)

SRV furnishes the most explicit and prescriptive statement of what a better life is, or is not, for people with intellectual disabilities. It involves promotion of 'valued social roles' including that of paid worker, author and citizen (Wolfensberger and Tullman, 1989); 'accomplishments' such as physical presence, choice, competence, respect and participation (O'Brien and Lyle, 1987). SRV set benchmarks on issues such as rights, individuality, social integration and typical patterns for living (Felce et al, 1998, p 11). This allowed for judgement on the extent to which services met the exacting standards of SRV, a practice facilitated by a comprehensive programme of training for professionals (PASS and PASSING), which was widely disseminated in the UK from the later 1970s (Lindley and Wainwright, 1992). SRV sought to promote positive imagery: 'as much as possible any features of human services that can convey image messages about clients at risk should be positive' (Wolfensberger and Tullman, 1989, p 217).

Thus SRV sought to outlaw practices such as siting facilities for 'the mentally handicapped' near cemeteries (association with death), displaying pictures of animals on walls (association with subhumans) and allowing people to behave in ways that were not age appropriate, for example carrying toys or comforters around (failure to enhance social role and competence). In this way the image of people was to be enhanced.

It is tempting to regard the ubiquitous glossy photos of well-dressed people with intellectual disabilities standing smiling in modern clean kitchens that adorn contemporary policy documents as direct descendants of Wolfensberger's precepts about positive imagery.

'Normalisation' and SRV became the dominant theoretical framework in the 1980s, and, we argue, have remained the underpinning assumption for service provision and for policy: 'People with intellectual disabilities are entitled to the same aspirations and life chances as other people' (DH, 2009, p 3).

There is much that is admirable in this determination to reverse the impact of whatever caused the 'learning disability' or 'special needs' label to be attached to the person. But it carries dangers. Joanna Ryan, writing in 1987, pointed out the implications:

> The historic concern with the human status of the mentally handicapped has become a concern with their normality – or at any rate, how normal they can be made ... many current proposals within the subnormality services and institutions are based upon the assumption that mentally handicapped people can lead a more normal life than was previously thought, or that they can be educated and trained to do so. (Ryan with Thomas, 1980, p 122)

Ryan's words alert us to one of the difficulties faced by writers and policy makers when they fail to consider fully what they are aiming for in terms of the lives of people with intellectual disabilities. There has been a drive to 'make' people normal, to 'insert' them into the mainstream of ordinary life, without really thinking through the consequences of this. Normalisation has been criticised for this, though it is only fair to say that Wolfensberger and others were very concerned to find ways to make 'communities' more welcoming, through, for example, citizen advocacy schemes, through encouraging staff to make their networks available to the people they worked with and for, and by encouraging mainstream services to adjust their approach to ensure people can be included. However there was a failure to consider whether people with intellectual disabilities as individuals wanted prescribed normalisation, or to think about the multifarious communities to which people could belong.

Normalisation/SRV owe much to Goffman's *Stigma*, which posits that a stigma, a digression from the norm, challenges the stigmatised person to manage social interactions in such a way as to reduce embarrassment. The onus is on the stigmatised person to do this (Goffman,1990). Social perceptions of the stigma lead to social devaluation, creating an inescapable cycle. There is a permanent and unbridgeable binary between the normal and the 'discredited' individual. Despite challenges to the concept of 'normal' by disabled academics (French, 1993), the premise posed by Goffman has remained as a fundamental underpinning assumption of a binary – there are disabled and non-disabled people. However successful people are in 'passing' as normal, or becoming accepted into the mainstream, or finding valued social roles, they remain, in this theory, stigmatised and disabled.

The centrality of stigma in the lives of people with intellectual disabilities was explored graphically by Robert Edgerton in his celebrated study, *The cloak of competence* (1967), of people who left a California institution in the 1960s. Edgerton was one of the first researchers to interview people with intellectual disabilities directly, to 'allow the mentally retarded to speak for themselves' as the book's jacket has it (1971 edition). But he heard their words and observed their lives through his own lens. The book's subtitle *Stigma in the lives of the mentally retarded*, gives a clue to his assumptions. Edgerton sees negotiating stigma as central:

> No one whose stigma is mental retardation jokes about it. For the accused or suspected mental retardate, passing and denial are as much a life and death matter as are the deception of a spy behind enemy lines. (1967, p 208)

Edgerton regarded the stigma as overwhelming, denying it, or passing, a matter of 'life and death'. He wrote: 'the mental retardate is *forever* doomed to his condition' (p 207). He allows for no alternatives, no escape, no statements that retardation is an alternative identity, to be celebrated rather than rejected:

> These former patients are not social deviants who have rejected the normative expectations of the 'outside' normal world. They espouse no counter-morality. Quite the contrary, their every effort is directed towards effecting a

legitimate entry into the 'outside' world. To do so they will lie and cheat, but they practice their deceptions in order to claim a place in the 'normal' world, not to deviate from it. (Edgerton, 1967, p 209)

For Edgerton, as for the overwhelming majority of academics and policy makers since, there is a binary, there are the 'retardates' or people with intellectual disabilities, and there is the normal world, and the task is one of facilitating entry into that world, and staying there, achieved by conforming, by learning its rules and by 'passing'. One might cast the panoply of legislation, charters and statements of rights as seeking to create the macrostructures that will facilitate this entry.

Thus normalisation can be interpreted in ways that minimise difference, leading to situations where 'significant impairments and the personal histories that produce human damage are not so much denied as glossed over' (Burton and Kagan, 2006, p 305). Inclusion is one way by which people with intellectual disabilities must travel into the communities of ordinary life, populated by non-disabled people. One author calls this 'insertion' (Winance, 2007). This can contribute (and, we would argue, has done so) to a situation in which vagueness about what inclusion in the community or an ordinary life is leads to unrealistic expectations in which responsibility for an undefined 'conformity' is placed on individuals with intellectual disabilities, and the staff who work with them, and which has inhibited a broad-ranging consideration of the nature of a good life, and how it might be achieved.

The social model of disability

Although we would argue that the social model of disability has been less influential than normalisation/social role valorisation in directly influencing provision and practice in intellectual disabilities, it has contributed powerfully to arguments for people being regarded as citizens, and has certainly contributed to the trend to wish away the impairment.

From the social model perspective, it is external barriers rather than bodily limitations that create oppression and prejudice, the actual impairment, it is argued, does not matter (Oliver, 1990). The extent to which the barriers to full societal participation can be reduced when the impairment is intellectual rather than physical is contestable, but rarely debated (Chappell, 1997; Shakespeare, 2006). Although it values the collective power of disabled people, the social model is predicated on an individualistic concept of human rights. Such individualised conceptions ill-serve some people with intellectual disabilities who will inevitably struggle in a world that pays little heed to their often very specific and conditional needs.

To the social model we owe ideas such as direct payments and individualised budgets, which put the service user in charge of employing their own support (Morris, 2004; Leece and Bornat, 2006). Such models have served some physically disabled people remarkably well (Campbell, 2006), and they have been systematically (if slowly) extended to other groups who require support. To the social model we also owe the rejection of 'care' as demeaning, to be substituted by personal assistance designed to 'take the place of my hands' (Meyer et al, 2007).

There are differences between normalisation and the social model of disability, and these have been well aired in the literature (see Walmsley, 2001). But there are also striking similarities. Both rely on creating binary categories without which they would have no meaning – there are disabled people and there are non-disabled people, and the categories are pretty watertight (Shakespeare, 2006). Both focus on the consequences, rather than the causes, specific experiences or nature, of the impairment. Both advocate social rather than medical intervention. And both argue, in different ways, that if only the environment were different, if attitudes and behaviours were to change, barriers were removed and systems were reformed, the impairment would matter less, if at all.

How do people with intellectual disabilities see their lives?

This chapter has so far recounted how ideas about changing the lives of people with intellectual disabilities for the better emerged from policy makers and theorists. These ideas belonged to family members, to professionals, researchers, campaigners and theorists, people speaking for people with intellectual disabilities. As had always been the case, the people themselves lacked a say, or, if they had one, it is not easy to access. Ironically much of what is documented still comes from non-disabled people, and therein lies a tension, which we explore below.

Speaking up by people with intellectual disabilities is dated as having its beginnings in Sweden in the late 1960s when, according to Goodley (2000), a small group of people put requests for improved services to the parent organisation that supported them. From the 1980s the voices of people with intellectual disabilities began to become louder, and have increasingly articulated ideas about the good life:

> From a substantial history of silence, people labelled as
> having a learning difficulty have in the last 30 years made
> substantial moves to have their voices heard, to reclaim their
> lives, and to take charge of their own destiny and identity.
> (Goodley and Ramcharan, 2005, p 150)

Marie's story is one of many examples of people speaking out and
having their accounts written down by others. The extent to which she
has been able to 'take charge of her own destiny' is questionable, though
there is clear evidence that she has found a voice that will reach many
people, and that she is able to articulate a far more complex identity
than the label 'intellectual disability' can convey.

Goodley and Ramcharan (2005) trace the development of people
with intellectual disabilities speaking out about their lives from tentative
beginnings to the present when, they propose, following Bersani (1998),
that self-advocacy (speaking up by people with intellectual disabilities)
might be considered to constitute a 'new social movement' in which:

- Members go beyond typical roles: for instance, from passive recipients
  of services to citizens, researchers, workers, campaigners, in other
  words adopting 'valued social roles'.
- Strong ideological change is represented: moving from a situation
  in which others speak for them, to speaking for themselves and
  articulating their own aspirations.
- A new identity emerges: for example, refining or redefining labels.
  The most salient example of this is the slogan 'label jars not people'
  adopted by People First (Goodley and Ramcharan, 2005), and the
  insistence (in the UK) on the term 'people with learning difficulties'
  rather than 'mental handicap', 'intellectual disability' or 'learning
  disability', the terms adopted by governments and services.
- Relationship between the movement and the individual is blurred:
  there is both individual and collective campaigning (adapted from
  Goodley and Ramcharan, 2005).

This analysis is an example of the resolute optimism not uncommon
in this field. It appears to be influenced by Wolfensberger's injunction
to convey positive messages, rather than being empirically grounded.
The literature on self-advocacy is with a few exceptions (Goodley,
2000; Clement, 2004; Chapman, 2005) remarkably light on empirical
research (Buchanan and Walmsley, 2006). The optimism is shared by
academic advocates without disabilities, and leading self-advocates alike.

So what does a 'good life' look like from the point of view of the people whose lives are in question? It is perhaps not surprising that the kinds of lives people have said they want match the expectations and the formulas of the policy makers. It is relatively easy to compile a list that resembles that of *Valuing people now* – a home, a job, good support, choice, independence. For example, the web page of People First London UK stated in November 2008:

> People First promotes the social model of disability. This is a way of thinking about disability that says it is society that needs to change to include disabled people. We should not have to change to fit in with society. We are against the medical model of disability, which is the view that being disabled means there is 'something wrong' with you. Doctors and teachers and other professionals put labels on us marking us out as different from everyone else.
>
> It is these labels which get in the way and stop us taking part the same as anyone else, for example people labelled as having a learning difficulty get sent to special schools and then on to day centres when what we would really like is to get a job; we get put in group homes to live with other people with the same label, with whom we didn't choose to live, when we would prefer to live on our own with support or with a boyfriend or girlfriend. (www.peoplefirstltd.com/)

Other than the issue of labelling, which is prominent for this group in a way that it is not in ministerial pronouncements, this statement echoes the *Valuing people* vision – a home of one's own, a job, use of the services everyone uses. Both parties agree that intellectual disability is a 'social' not a 'health' or medical issue.

People First's statement lays a great deal of blame for their oppression and lack of a good life on labels. Labels lead to special schooling and day centres, which, it is implied, stand in the way of people getting the jobs they want. Labels lead to people being put into group homes, when they really want to live on their own, with support and a partner or lover. It is striking, despite the overt espousal of the 'social model' of disability, how much this analysis owes to Wolfensberger who stated:

> It is a well established fact that a person's behavior tends to be profoundly affected by the role expectations placed upon him ... this permits those who define social roles to make self fulfilling prophecies. (Wolfensberger et al, 1972, pp 15–16)

Brown and Smith (1992) observe that Wolfensberger was influenced by labelling theories fashionable in the 1960s, which argued that it was labels and their consequences rather than any 'biological or psychological factors' (p 6) that may have led to the labelling. The theory behind this owes a great deal to Goffman's concept of stigma discussed earlier in this chapter. It is remarkable that 30 years on such ideas continue to surface, unquestioned, in the manifestos of campaigning groups. Why the labels are attached is not discussed, although it is implied that this is a professional conspiracy, the work of 'doctors and teachers'.

In the USA, the SABE (Self Advocates Become Empowered) website lays out its priorities:

1. Eliminate institutions;
2. SABE will support affordable and accessible housing for all people in the community;
3. National healthcare for all people;
4. Equal employment opportunities for equal pay for all people;
5. People with disabilities will have self-advocacy at all stages of their lives with funding to support state, local and national self-advocacy organizations;
6. SABE will educate people with and without disabilities on the options, choices and alternatives to guardianship so that full guardianship is not an option whenever possible;
7. Relationships;
8. SABE will be a political powerhouse to work on legislation that effects people with disabilities lives;
9. SABE will advocate for individualized services for all people with disabilities;
10. SABE will support flexible and available accessible transportation (airlines, trains, buses) for all people in the community across the nation; and,
11. SABE will educate people – all people – about disability issues that are important in their lives. (www.sabeusa. org/)

There are similarities here with the manifesto of People First London in the emphasis on home and work, choice and control, though this manifesto lacks the sophisticated labelling underpinning theory articulated by the London-based organisation.

What if we look beyond the words of the activists, if we listen with care to disentangle what is really important for people to feel they are living a 'good life'? Of course, with a very heterogeneous group, there will be no simple answers – personalised response is vital.

We have used Marie Wolfe's story throughout the book to illustrate the individualism and complexities inherent in enabling a good life. In a remarkably honest account of her work as a paid supporter in an independent self-advocacy organisation, Tricia Webb pondered what it would mean to listen behind the lines. She embarked on writing a chapter for an edited book *Therapy and intellectual disabilities* (1999), and chose to base this on interviews with three people she knew well. She describes reflecting on her interview notes thus:

> Looking at my notes, afterwards, there seemed to be something lacking, something rather impersonal and even clinical about what I had written. I realised that I had managed to confine all 3 people to talking about the things I felt that I already knew ... my paper was full of comments like 'people don't listen to what I want', 'professionals never have time for me' ... 'they try to run my life for me' ... I had unconsciously set myself in the role of expert ... I had created a caricature of people with intellectual disabilities and learned nothing new. (Webb, 1999, pp 47–8)

Webb points to a real danger of some of the rhetoric that currently shapes policies and ideas about the lives of people with intellectual disabilities. It fails to get behind the jargon of choice, rights and independence, to delve into what is really important to people – and what might be achievable. The jargon conveniently hides resource implications in demanding that people have the lives others lead as of right, manna from heaven to politicians and service providers looking for quick and inexpensive wins. Rhetoric from academics, advocates and campaigning groups can paradoxically play into the hands of those who wish to minimise and simplify a complex set of problems (Burton and Kagan, 2006; Dowse, 2009). The road to hell is paved with good intentions.

The lives that people lead

Empirical evidence indicates that, behind the rhetoric, life for many people with intellectual disabilities is grim. A report on the government-funded first national survey of adults with intellectual disabilities published on 28 September 2005 by the Health and Social Care Information Centre completed by BMRB, Lancaster University and Central England People First offers a more comprehensive picture of the extent to which 'a good life' had been achieved. The Lancaster University Press Release summarises the findings:

> We interviewed just under 3,000 people with intellectual disabilities to find out what their life is like, including where they live and with whom, what they do during the day and what are their needs, wants and aspirations. We also collected views on the support received by individuals.
>
> The results highlight the extent of hardship and social exclusion faced by people with intellectual disabilities in terms of material hardship, employment opportunities and social participation. They also highlight how little control many people with intellectual disabilities have over important aspects of their lives, for example, who they live with and where they live.
>
> The results show that some people with intellectual disabilities are more likely to be socially excluded and face adversity than others. People with intellectual disabilities from poorer backgrounds and from minority ethnic communities are particularly at risk.
>
> They tell us how much more needs to be done if people with intellectual disabilities are to 'be respected and included as equal members of society' – the 2025 objective in *Improving the life chances of disabled people*. (Lancaster University, 2007)

The conclusion reached by the research team was that a substantial proportion of those interviewed were socially excluded, but, above all, that they were poor. Poverty appeared to exacerbate the likelihood of living in a poor neighbourhood, a sense of loneliness and the likelihood of being a victim of crime and bullying.

The survey was completed around 25 years after the bold aspirations for an ordinary life were first articulated. Yet the evidence indicates that for people without family or benefactors life could be quite bleak. As Pam Dale put it:

> Worklessness, in an age when citizenship is all too often conditional on a relationship to paid employment, and the resulting poverty and forced recourse to the public

authorities for assistance form a rather uncomfortable thread between past and present. (Dale, 2008, p 73)

The role of labelling was not highlighted in the National Survey. Without some form of labelling, the survey would not have been possible. But placing the blame on labels is an inadequate response.

It is not to be wondered at that policy articulated by politicians, academics and self-advocates alike places paid employment at the centre of the web of initiatives to help people to a good life. Without private resources from family or friends, paid work is the only real alternative to poorly funded public services. There has, as we will show in Chapter Six, been a longer history than is often realised of initiatives to ensure that people with intellectual disabilities 'pay their way', from work in institutions, to farm work and domestic labour, to contract work in Adult Training Centres. Yet unless employers become ready to accommodate difference, to provide skilled support and to override the accepted skills and qualifications thresholds for employment, it is likely that those who find jobs will be confined to low-paid and unskilled roles; while for a substantial majority, including those above retirement age and those whose needs are profound, multiple or complex, paid employment will be an impossible aspiration. And if this is achieved, what is the point of the label 'intellectual disabilities'?

Conclusion

In all the policy rhetoric about the lives of people with intellectual disabilities a good life rarely features. In spite of the positive spin given to the mantras that head government policies they suggest both a lack of clarity and definition in their aims, which is then translated into practice. Not many people would argue against the view that people with intellectual disabilities want a life like any other, or an ordinary life, or that they need to be 'valued people'. But it is not possible to really know what these terms mean. We find it sad that these are flags waved by government policies.

From policy makers, theorists and self-advocates the cry and sometimes the plea is for equal access, and a lack of labels. The latter is particularly paradoxical since government policies depend on the binary of disabled–non-disabled for both their ideas and the resulting practices. The failure to define further what an ordinary life or a life like any other might mean leads in our view to a focus on the concrete and material in people's lives. We do not find this surprising since these are the easiest things to deal with if one is not focusing on the internal worlds of people.

Would the slogan 'a good life' be an advance on an 'ordinary life', or a 'life like any other'? Not, we would argue, if it becomes yet another simplistic mantra. If we take a 'good life' seriously, we'll need to ponder what it might mean to balance freedom with constraint, consider duty and virtue alongside the pursuit of pleasure, and address the implications of impaired reason. We need to recognise that impaired reason will compromise the extent to which some people with intellectual disabilities can enter the social contract on equal terms. For some, it may be possible, with appropriate support, to get a job, run a home, raise children and so fulfil some of the criteria that our society values. For others, even the most skilled support is unlikely to achieve those goals without massive changes in the wider society. The challenge is to incorporate the ideas articulated in this book about a good life into thinking about ways better lives can be achieved for all, even with the most profound impairments; to enabling people, and those who care for and about them, to work out for themselves what a good life might mean.

FIVE

Changing problems, changing solutions

This chapter continues the theme of Part Two, tracing how we got to where we are today. In this chapter we examine changing assumptions about intellectual disability and their implications for a good life. In particular we explore how intellectual disability has been variously constructed as a problem and how 'solutions' to it have changed over time. We argue that despite dramatic changes in the way intellectual disability has been constructed since the early 20th century, there are continuities also, in the form of the creation of a binary – us and them – and a wish to diminish or minimise the costs associated with supporting adults who are rarely able to be financially self-supporting, and that 'they' constitute a perceived problem for which a solution has to be found. As a result of this, we argue that it is hardly surprising that a good life for people with intellectual disabilities has not been at the forefront of society's planning and practice in relation to them.

Chapter Four provided an account of how policy has evolved to the point where a 'better life' is equated with individualism, and, as Burton and Kagan put it, 'significant impairments and the personal histories that produce human damage are not so much denied as glossed over' (2006, p 305). There is a paradox here. As we have shown in Part One, contemporary views of a good life, in part, have been premised on values of autonomy, equality and participation. The fact that some adults require care underpins their exclusion from conventional conceptualisations of a good life. And yet, in spite of a failure to systematically define a good life, current policy across the English-speaking world now asserts the relevance of these values to the lives of people with intellectual disabilities.

In this chapter we argue that over the past 50 years, roughly the second half of the 20th century, ideas about people with intellectual disabilities shifted dramatically. From being a burden on society, they have become in rhetoric people to whom society owes a duty to provide at least some of the current values of a 'good life'. It is a pendulum swing that rehabilitated them from being constructed as a dangerous and burdensome group, to being presented as individuals with 'rights'. Assumptions about the nature of the problem learning disability presents, and the solutions, have also swung, each new solution premised on discrediting the past. The chapter examines these changes, on the premise that a consideration of the past can enable us to understand better the strengths and limitations of our contemporary blinkers. To do this it uses a framework borrowed from the literature on evaluation, a theory of change. This approach seeks to lay out assumptions about the nature of a social problem, what its solution is and how particular action will lead to the solution. It is a useful device to explore the shift from segregation and institutionalisation, to care in the mid-20th century, and then to what we have today – rights, choice, inclusion and personalisation. It leads to a critical re-evaluation of some taken-for-granted assumptions that have determined thinking about what constitutes a good life, and how it should be achieved.

The chapter is not a defence of the indefensible, not a rallying cry for a return to the old abusive institutions. But it does seek to demonstrate that institutions were not the only problem, nor is deinstitutionalisation the only answer; and that normalisation/social role valorisation and the social model may have taken us as far as they can.

Stage 1: finding a solution for the burden of 'mental deficiency'

Until the middle of the 20th century there was little challenge to the belief that had prevailed since its first decade, that people with intellectual disabilities were at best people to be cared for and protected and at worst people who threatened the social order. Early in the 20th century, legislation was passed in most Western countries, plus Australasia, which sought to isolate people with intellectual disabilities ('mental defectives' or 'feeble-minded' in contemporary terminology), to control them and, above all, to prevent them breeding (Jackson, 2001). For the most part, this control was to be exercised through placing people who were deemed to be mentally deficient in institutions, often for long periods. It was also exercised through close surveillance of families where there was a 'mental defective' (Rolph and Walmsley, 2001), and through sterilisation, both formally approved through law (as in Denmark, Sweden and many US states) (Park and Radford, 1998) and informally without legal sanction, according to oral history evidence from former residents in the United Kingdom and Australia (Johnson et al, 2001).

The intended outcome of these policies was that social problems would be reduced and that, by the prevention of 'breeding', the quality of the population would improve (Jones, 1986).

Assumptions about the nature of the problem

Segregation was adopted as a solution because people labelled as 'feeble-minded' were seen as a problem group, responsible for a range of social ills. The fashionable pseudo-science of eugenics had led to a concern at the proliferation of the working class, particularly its less respectable members, at the expense of 'better stocks' (Jones, 1986, p 18). The 'feeble-minded' were described as 'the menace of the feebleminded' (Trent, 1994, Ch 5). Alfred Tredgold, a commentator of the time, listed the following social problems attributable to these individuals:

- abnormally fertile women who gave birth to defective children like themselves;
- illegitimacy;
- the spread of venereal disease;
- criminality;
- pauperism; and
- drunkenness.

For Tredgold, 'the feeble minded and their relatives form a very considerable proportion, if not the whole, of the social failures and the degenerates of the nation' (quoted in Jones, 1986, p 94).

The solution to this problem was to identify and isolate these people, and prevent their breeding. Campaigns by the National Association for the Care of the Feeble Minded (founded 1896) and the Eugenics Education Society (founded 1907) pressed for such solutions based on either segregation or sterilisation. They were successful in provoking a Royal Commission, which pronounced in 1908. Its conclusions were that there was a case for legislation.

The campaigns for legislation were built on fear, and the predominant arguments were couched in terms of the need to protect society from the menace of the feeble-minded. Legislation passed in the UK in 1913 provided for institutional care for 'mental defectives', and although this only ever included a proportion of those who were ascertained as 'feeble-minded', the principles of control and stigmatisation were enshrined in law. This discourse was barely challenged for 50 years. Much later, in 1943, the purpose of services is succinctly described by Rex Blake Marsh, the Medical Superintendent of Bromham House, a medium-sized English Mental Deficiency Hospital, who repeated the words of the 1932 Ray Committee in his introduction to the Bromham Annual Report in 1943:

> The primary purpose of the service should be the protection of the public against defectives who may be a danger to the community. The second should be the maintenance of these and other mental defectives in reasonable circumstances.

He goes on to point out that:

> consideration should be given to the needs of the fit at whose cost they must be supported. (Blake Marsh, 1943, p 3)

These views prevailed into the early 1950s. The 1952 edition of the leading British textbook on mental deficiency, by the same Alfred Tredgold, stated:

> The 80,000 or more idiots and imbeciles in the country … are not only incapable of being employed to any economic advantage, but their care and support, whether in their own homes or in institutions, absorbs a large amount of time, energy and money of the normal population which could be used for better purposes. (Tredgold, 1952, quoted in Emerson et al, 2005, p 113)

He goes on to use phrases including 'utterly helpless, repulsive in appearance and revolting in manners' (p 113). Clearly, in such a world view, a good life was not on the agenda – or was premised for others on getting rid of this enormous burden.

That Tredgold continued with a refrain he began before 1908 indicates that the solution had not worked – indeed, the words he uses are telling – however they were catered for, whether in families or institutions, the burden persisted.

The institutional regime that was put in place in all Western countries during the early 20th century, a regime that segregated people for long periods, even for life, if they appeared to pose any threat to the community, was little challenged until around the end of the Second World War (Stainton, 2000). Given the often draconian practices, with individuals taken into institutional care in childhood, frequently subject to a lifetime of incarceration, this is a matter of surprise, as Stainton notes. The institutional solution had not delivered a solution, or possibly the solution was at too high a cost. At the time Tredgold's words were published, change was, finally, in the air.

Metzel sees the catalyst for change as 'the profound public and systematic failure of the institutions', hastened by parent advocacy, judicial activism, legislative action, costs and the acceptance of the ideology of normalisation (2004, p 434). Public scandals about abuse in institutions were a precursor to their becoming seen as the cause of problems, rather than the solution they were originally designed to be.

Arguably, institutions were discredited not only because 'batch living' (Goffman, 1968) went out of fashion in a world of possessive individualism, but also because of the expense of maintaining high-quality environments. Institutions failed in part because they were poorly maintained, under-resourced and staffed by people lacking in imagination and training, and, sometimes, in compassion.

Michael McFadden, a nurse employed at Lennox Castle Hospital in Scotland, reflected on the changes during his working life:

> When Lennox Castle opened in '36 it was heralded as the best example of care for the mentally deficient in Britain. People came from all over to see it ... so everyone thought that was the best thing.... Everybody thought 'we are providing the best care that can be provided.' It's a question of evolution; time has moved. I think there's no doubt that it was the best example of care available, but instead of maybe moving forward and maybe embracing new ideas as they came, I think the hospital probably did – and I would be part of it – stagnate somewhat in the 50s, 60s and 70s. (McFadden, 2002)

Community care, the proposed alternative, 'allowed governments to save money while simultaneously giving their policy a humanitarian gloss' (Scull, 1984, p 139).

We argued in introducing this section that the problem to which institutional care was the intended solution was the threat posed by the 'feeble-minded' as the cause of social ills and degeneracy. Institutional care, however, brought its own problems of cost and quality, as well as challenges on moral grounds. Nor had it delivered the expected outcome. Over half a century of institutional policies had not eliminated social ills. As institutions went out of vogue, so the problem was reframed.

Stage 2: the problem reframed as family burden

The second stage of change was framed around creating support in the 'community', alongside institutions. The problem was reframed to be the threat to family life posed by people with 'mental retardation' (US) (Castles, 2004), or 'subnormals' (UK) (Welshman, 2006), and the burden they imposed on their families. The solution was to be 'community care'.

Challenges to the negativity that had prevailed in the first half of the 20th century began to be launched in the late 1940s by parents' groups, which had recently formed, by the National Council for Civil Liberties and by some in authority in services (Stainton, 2000). Similar developments occurred more or less simultaneously in the Nordic countries, in Canada, the USA and in Australia (Castles, 2004; Jones, 2004; Johnson and Traustadottir, 2005; Stainton, 2006; Tøssebro, 2006; Trent, 2006).

The UK National Council for Civil Liberties (NCCL) launched a campaign against some of the excesses of institutional care in a pamphlet *50,000 Outside the Law* in 1951. Their argument for change is couched in an appeal to our shared humanity. By the standards of the 21st century it reads as somewhat paternalistic, but, nevertheless, is an important articulation of the underpinning of the 'good life', an assertion of common humanity:

> The idiot, the imbecile and feebleminded are an integral part of the human race; their existence constitutes an important demand upon us. The extent to which we guard their right to the fullest and most useful life, the extent to which we guarantee them the maximum freedom which they can enjoy and the extent to which we help their families to give them the love they need is a measure of the extent to which we ourselves are civilized. (NCCL, 1951, quoted in Stainton, 1994, p 132)

The NCCL's campaign reframes the problem. No longer are people with intellectual disabilities a burden, rather they are a moral obligation on others, to optimise freedom and access to a full and useful life, and to support families. This was one of the first modern manifestations of the view that the issues framing the lives of people with intellectual disabilities is one of human rights (Stainton, 2000), and that society, rather than needing to be protected, has a duty to foster a better life.

However, without other developments this might have remained an isolated campaign. One of the most significant changes in the mid-20th century was the advent of parents' groups. This was a common phenomenon across Western countries at this time (see Trent, 1994; Welshman and Walmsley, 2006), and appears to be the first time that 'consumers' as opposed to 'do-gooders' grouped together as pressure groups for change (see Rolph, 2000; Walmsley, 2000). Rolph speculates on the reasons for this emergence in the UK of what are now familiar models of voluntary bodies, comprising self-help along with campaigning and, in some cases, service provision. She links it to the advent of the welfare state. However, this happened at a similar time in the US (Trent, 1994), where there was no welfare state, with celebrities such as cowboy film star Dale Rogers 'coming out' (Trent, 1994) about their handicapped children, as did (now Lord) Brian Rix, comic actor, in England (Shennan, 1980). Jones (2004, p 326) observes that:

> Notions of the public 'menace of the feeble minded' popular in the early years of the twentieth century had largely dissipated by the post war years, only to be replaced by fears of mental retardation as the destroyer of family harmony.

She points out that some families, including prominent psychologist Erik Erikson, chose to exclude and deny their child with intellectual disability, while others began to claim public recognition that 'having a retarded child is not a disgrace, and that they can be assisted and that they are entitled to aid' (*New York Times*, quoted in Jones, 2004, p 327). Castles states that between 1946 and 1950 no fewer than 77 parents' groups were founded in the USA. A similar phenomenon can be seen in England where 200 branches of the National Association of Parents of Backward Children (NAPBC) were started between 1947 and 1956 (Shennan, 1980; Rolph et al, 2005).

As Jones and Rolph show in relation to the US and UK, respectively, these parents' groups began to articulate demands for a better life for their children based on entitlement. Both in the US and the UK, access to education was at the heart of the demands made by parents' groups. While campaigning for policy change, some Local Societies took steps to fill in the enormous gaps in community provision. Bedford's NAPBC branch, for example, was founded in 1955 (Rolph et al, 2005). Brenda Nickson, a founder member of Bedford's Society, commented in an interview with the author, conducted in 2000, that the Society's early aim was 'to try and get people to treat our people as though there was at least a certain amount of normality. They were all human beings' (Nickson, 2005, p 78).

This Society instituted in the 1950s and 1960s home visitors for new parents, nursery schools, holidays in a chalet bought for the purpose and a community cafe (Rolph et al, 2005). The parties and fund-raising activities undertaken by such parents' groups enabled these 'less than normal' families to create a semblance of normal life for themselves, and their offspring (Jones, 2004).

Self-help only went so far in satisfying these newly mobilised families. Jones (2004) explains how schooling became the rallying point in New Jersey. Using the slogan 'For every child a fair chance' (p 339), legislation was passed in that state in 1954 mandating schools to provide classes for 'trainable' children. In the UK, although the initial focus was on education for children, local groups also campaigned, often successfully, for facilities for adults, such as Adult Training Centres, to be provided by the local authority during the 1950s (Rolph, 2002).

The UK national umbrella organisation, the NAPBC, later Mencap, contributed, for example, to the Royal Commission on the law relating to mental illness and mental deficiency (1954–57), the first time 'consumers' had been party to national policy making in this field (Welshman, 2006).

Parents' groups were successful in reframing the problem of mental deficiency from one associated with 'Genetic degeneracy ... low social class, sexual misbehaviour, criminal tendencies' (Castles, 2004, p 352), to one that could affect any family. Walmsley writes of the English NAPBC as:

> a forum in which parents of sons and daughters with a learning disability began to represent their private interests in and to the public world. Their role was to challenge the way public services were provided and demand a better deal for members and their children. (2000, p 104)

The US equivalent, the Association for the Help of Retarded Children, used associations with children with physical disabilities, such as polio, to foster public support and understanding (Castles, 2004). They, like their UK equivalent, also fostered the 'eternal child' image, using appealing, mildly disabled children in poster campaigns. This not only enhanced their public acceptance, it also placed families in an unassailable position as spokespersons and advocates for 'children who never grew' (Castles, 2004, p 360). From being a problem that required institutional solutions, intellectual disability was, in the quarter-century following the Second World War, framed as a problem affecting whole families, which required the community to change and adapt to welcome them and their children, as Castles points out, implicitly challenging the idea that problem and solution 'could be found in the disabled individual alone' (2004, p 364) and calling into question the medical model.

At the same time as parents' groups in the UK and the US began to articulate demands for acceptance as 'human beings', as Brenda Nickson (2005) put it, and the services to go with it, provision, often meagre and of poor quality, began to be provided in 'the community'. These developments increased the visibility of 'mental deficiency', and enabled more connections to be forged between parents.

Stage 3: the solution to the problem – 'community care'

The campaigning undertaken by parents' organisations was a contributor to developments in policy known as 'community care'. 'Community care' began to become official policy in aspiration in the UK in the late 1950s (Mental Health Act 1959). As an adjunct to institutions, it had been in existence since the early part of the 20th century (Rolph and Walmsley, 2001). In the second half of the 20th century it became seen as a superior alternative to, and, later, a replacement for, institutional care (Means et al, 2003; Walmsley, 2006).

This was the start of a pendulum swing away from regarding institutions as a solution to seeing them as the source of oppression. Andrew Scull, historian of mental health in the UK, commented:

> From the mid-1950s onwards our own generation has embraced with equal foolishness the contention that ... the worst home is better than the best mental hospital. (Scull, 1996, p 13)

In the somewhat vitriolic chapter from which this quotation is taken, Scull castigates the discrediting of the concept of 'asylum', and points to the remarkable change from institutional care to community care as the preferred care environment in mental health. He overstates his case. The process, in our view, took far longer, but if he overstated his case, we would propose that this is now the dominant view. Large institutions have been comprehensively discredited. Inclusion in communities is regarded as the only proper way for people to live (see, for example, DH, 2001, 2009).

It is not possible here to tell the story of community care with all its subtleties, and the job has been done elsewhere (Trent, 1994; Means et al, 2003; Welshman and Walmsley, 2006). As Webster pertinently observed, 'because each new administration has adopted the idea as if it was its own discovery, introducing changes of meaning to suit the prevailing ideology, the extent of the longer term preoccupation with community care tends to be obscured' (Webster, 1996, p 109). In some respects the ideas and idealism of activists has been made to serve the baser interests of politicians to cut costs and reduce dependence on the welfare agencies.

The view that care in the community was superior to, and should replace, institutional care emerged slowly from around the mid-1950s, as we have shown. Initially, arguments for the development of community facilities were that they should be an adjunct to hospital care. Welshman (2006) traces this development to a constellation of factors, including campaigning by voluntary groups, but also cost factors and the work of academics such as Jack Tizard who, in a number of studies undertaken in the 1950s and 1960s, demonstrated that the existing system of care was flawed, that institutions were unsuitable environments and that people with intellectual disabilities had the potential to become successful in employment if given a positive environment and training. Of particular interest for our purpose of tracing how an ordinary life became a goal is the work of Clarke and Hermelin published in 1955: 'it seems that the limits to the trainability of imbeciles are very much higher than have been accepted traditionally either in theory or in practice' (quoted in Welshman and Walmsley, 2006, pp 27-8).

The process of moving from a view of mental deficiency as a fixed unalterable condition to a far more optimistic one of infinite potential, given the right attitudes and environment, had begun. Research began to dismantle eugenic assumptions, and show that, given the right environment, people could learn, and even those with very limited intelligence could sometimes be taught to perform useful work and satisfy the requirements of an industrial contractor (O'Connor and Tizard, 1954). Work as a desirable goal, and the persistent argument for enlightenment leading to lower costs of care, had already made its appearance.

Community provision was not entirely new in the post-Second World War era. Some English local authorities such as Somerset (Atkinson, 1997a) had had quite extensive provision of Occupation Centres by the late 1920s. However, less energetic areas had had little or nothing (French, 1971; Atkinson, 1997b; Humber, in press). It was claimed that community provision rapidly began to make inroads into hospital waiting lists (French, 1971), but, perhaps more importantly for our purpose here, such facilities brought what was then called 'mental deficiency' a little more into public view, and brought families into contact with one another, albeit in a limited way. This facilitated more contact between families, and was accentuated once schooling began to be provided for all (in the UK after 1970). Indeed two parent activists went so far as to argue that access to schooling was the biggest force for change as it meant 'mental handicap' became visible beyond the confines of segregated institutions even if it was only seeing people get onto (segregated) buses. They argued that, as a consequence, institutions became economically unviable. Michael Tombs, one of these activists, commented on how this had led to the undermining of the case for institutional care:

> To my mind, the key event of the last 50 years has been the opening of schools for children ... people started to keep their children at home with them, rather than put them in an institution ... with the hospitals not getting any new admissions, the numbers started to go down and the cost per head went up very sharply. (Tombs and Tombs, 2005, p 282)

At this time work in the UK indicated that care modelled on 'family' lines was ideologically preferred, in line with the parents' organisations' espousal of the 'eternal child' image. The ideology underpinning these early Occupation Centres is discussed by Rolph (2005b) who gives some useful insights, drawing on her oral history work with parents' groups in East Anglia, England. The model in force appears to have been modelled on schools with term times adhered to, and words like 'curriculum' used in inspectors' reports, though this curriculum was very limited, manual training and craftwork being predominant (Read and Walmsley, 2006).

The modelling of day services as providing for quasi-children is echoed by the practice of appointing married couples as 'house parents' when hostels began to open in the 1960s and 1970s. As the 1971 White Paper 'Better Services for the Mentally Handicapped' (England and Wales) put it, homes were to be encouraged to create a family atmosphere (Welshman, 2006, p 74). Research sponsored by the NAPBC, such as The Brooklands Experiment, supervised by Jack Tizard, was to support the need for 'care in small family groups' (Shennan, 1980, p 16).

This seems a long way from our earlier discussion of what might constitute a good life. At this point in time care and protection was afforded to people as if they were quasi-children, cared for in their families, or in residential care that provided a family atmosphere, offering, ideally close by, opportunities for sheltered employment or daytime activity (Welshman, 2006). This view, warmly espoused by many parents and the organisations they set up (Rolph et al, 2005), indicates the 'tension that is so often apparent with the family as both principal supporter but also principal restrictors of freedom' (Mitchell, 2006, p 124).

Deinstitutionalisation: A further solution

The model of the institution as the fundamental form of care provision took time to vanish. Until the later 1970s, reform was seen as developing community facilities alongside improved hospital provision (Malin et al, 1980; Welshman, 2006), to reform, not to replace, them. Increasingly, however, institutions came to be regarded as the source of the problem (Morris, 1969; Ryan with Thomas, 1987). The dismantling of institutional care and its replacement by community-based facilities was a prerequisite for a better life conceptualised as akin to a life led by ordinary, non-disabled people. By no stretch of the imagination, became the contention, could such a life be led in large institutions. People First Canada put it thus:

> But we cannot be citizens of this country and certainly cannot exercise our rights as citizens if we are locked up in institutions. (www.peoplefirstofcanada.ca/deinstitutionalization_en.php)

In making this statement they are echoing a discourse that brooks no disagreement.

One might go so far as to suggest that deinstitutionalisation is seen as the cure for disability. It sometimes seems to be conveniently believed that if you get rid of the institutions, you get rid of the perceived 'problem' posed by people with intellectual disabilities (Johnson and Traustadottir, 2005; Walmsley, 2005). There is no defending what institutions were and became with poor funding and low aspirations. However, there is a case for recognising that every generation has sought to find its own solutions to the challenge presented by adults unable to care for themselves, and that some genuinely believed that institutions were indeed preferable to the alternative – neglect (Jones, 1960).

By locating services and supports 'in the community', it was anticipated that magic would be wrought, inclusion in the lives and valued experiences of non-disabled people would follow. This premise we now know was deeply flawed – life in the 21st-century community was found to be impoverished, lonely and, frequently, unsafe unless family or friends were on hand (Emerson et al, 2005).

Phase 3: the problem reframed as denial of human rights attributable to labelling and social barriers

During the final quarter of the 20th century thinking changed again. From seeing the problem as the threat to family life created by the burden of what increasingly began to be called 'learning disability' (UK) or intellectual disability (US, Australia), under the influence of normalisation/SRV and, later, the social model of disability (see Chapter Four), the problem was recast as one of countering stigma and reducing barriers to participation as equal citizens. The solution adopted by our own generation has been to dismantle institutions of all kinds, not only the hospitals, but also day centres and sites of communal living. They are to be replaced with individually framed packages of care, in theory designed to provide people with a generalised version of a life like any other. Although in practice the family has provided continuing support for a large percentage of people with intellectual disabilities, it has in much policy rhetoric been cast aside – no longer the solution, but part of the problem. Families have been cast as 'overprotective' (Rolph et al, 2005), or even abusive.

The articulation of an ordinary life as the major policy goal can be dated to the 1970s as explained in Chapter Four:

> We can see the early 1970s as a watershed, the time when policy makers adopted the relatively optimistic ideas associated with researchers, mainly psychologists, who made the case for regarding people with mental handicaps as able to benefit from a comfortable environment, contact with the wider world, and education. (Welshman, 2006, p 17)

The reasons for this shift have been in part explored in Chapter Four, including powerful and attractive theories – normalisation/SRV and the social model of disability. Normalisation/SRV provided the rallying cry and a humane rationale across the West for closure of the large 20th-century colonies, which fitted neatly with other impetuses for change related to costs, difficulties of adequately staffing them and more fundamental shifts in the locus of responsibility for social care, moving away from the state to the individual and his or her family. To social role valorisation we can attribute current policies of mainstreaming in education, inclusion in mainstream health services, closure of large day centres and the pious hope that our precarious communities can somehow transform into utopias that include everyone.

The influence of the social model of disability thinking, which started with people with physical impairments, has more recently been applied to people with cognitive impairments: mental health problems, dementia and intellectual disabilities. Its emphasis on citizenship rather than care as the proper goal, on reducing external barriers to participation and on reclaiming a positive sense of identity as an oppressed minority (Oliver, 1990) has been influential in moving the debate on from the somewhat paternalistic vision of an ordinary life articulated by parents' groups in the mid-20th century to a more individualised rights-based discourse.

The solution: individualised funding and the market

The failure of state-provided community care solutions to provide a good-enough life, and to reduce costs, not to mention continuing scandals of abuse in these smaller establishments (Healthcare Commission, 2005, 2007), led to market-based individualised solutions to be advocated. This has resulted in governments advocating 'personalisation', a model of care that transfers purchasing power from service delivery agencies to individual users and their families (Duffy, 2006). This is expected to facilitate choice and control.

Personalisation, the transfer of employment from agencies to individuals, is regarded as a key to transformation from a service-dominated to a user-responsive service (Duffy, 2006). If, the argument goes, people who use services are to control what they get, then being able to select and direct staff will provide the solution.

The vision is one of integrated holistic services supporting independent living. Simon Duffy argued for self-directed support to be the norm. He proposed that the system of social care is inherently wasteful, both of resources and of people's lives. Resources are directed to services, not people. It generates costs of assessment, management and profit for private providers, and does not provide what people want for themselves.

Self-directed support, he claimed, in which users/patients control the resources allocated to them, will save money, both by making savings on overhead costs and by making better use of community resources – he cited the example of transport. Instead of special buses that waste time and money, people will make their own choices, and use their money wisely to access the transport of their choice.

Duffy's view is that self-directed support will enable disabled people to play a fuller part in society, and contribute to the acquisition of resources as well as consuming them because it can be used to support employment, volunteering and other socially useful activity.

Unusually, people with intellectual disabilities were in the vanguard of individualised budget implementation. The campaign led by Duffy's organisation, In Control, to implement personalised budgets was adopted into policy in 2007. All English local authorities were to offer a personal budget to everyone who wanted one (DH, 2007a).

The evidence for the extent to which this transfer of economic resources does deliver a better life to service users is limited. The claims made by Duffy were largely borne out in an evaluation of In Control's second phase by Professor Chris Hatton published in 2008 (see www.in-control.org.uk/site/INCO/UploadedResources/0550_Phase_Two_Report.pdf.pdf).

Of the people who used personal budgets, 196 were interviewed, and most reported improvements in quality of life, choice and control, spending time with people they like and personal dignity (Hatton, 2008). Hatton also noted that where friends and family were intimately involved, outcomes were likely to be improved.

However, it is too early to be certain that such a transfer will result in a good life for all service users. Having supportive family and friends emerged in Hatton's research as an important condition for improved satisfaction in this system. There has to date been relatively little rigorous research into the nature of the relationship between people with intellectual disabilities and the personal assistants they employ. Some studies of personal assistant schemes have begun to emerge, and these are discussed in depth later in this book. There is some worrying evidence that these reforms only reach some people. Others, those with more profound impairments, those with 'dual diagnosis' and those whose behaviour presents a challenge to staff, continue to be placed out of sight in euphemistically named 'out of area placements' (Beadle-Brown et al, 2005). Just as long-stay hospitals coexisted with community care, so institutional solutions persist alongside the personalised agenda.

Moreover, it is important to note that in debates around the implementation of personal budgets, some concerns have been raised. Staff terms and conditions may be less favourable than in traditionally delivered services, and one type of oppression, of service users, may be replaced by the oppression of staff. Jan Leece (2006), in an early study of personal assistants, noted higher levels of job satisfaction than in traditional home carer roles, but lower pay and less clarity over boundaries. Issues such as who pays when the assistant accompanies the service user to a leisure activity of their choice have begun to be raised on email list servers, with no clear answer emerging.

Further there are new and complex relationships in this new paradigm. In England, the debate has focused on whether personal assistants should have Criminal Record Bureau checks, and whether they should be subject to inspection by the state regulatory body, the Care Quality Commission. Given the drive in the independent living movement to deprofessionalise and demedicalise the personal assistant role, this threat to the ability of service user employers to employ whomever they choose has been vehemently resisted. It does not require a great deal of imagination, however, to appreciate that people with intellectual disabilities, and others who may lack agency and supportive personal networks, could be highly vulnerable to abuse at the hands of unscrupulous personal assistants, just as they were and are to staff employed in more traditional services. Anecdotal evidence suggests that this can be the case. 'Danny' was an active member of a self-advocacy group when living in a group home. He suddenly stopped attending when he moved into his own rented flat with an assistant he employed directly. When the self-advocacy support worker inquired why, he informed her that the assistant preferred shopping to taking him to the group (personal communication, 2008).

Raising questions about the direction of travel to individualised and personalised care, with paid work as the key goal, is difficult. The pendulum swing has been so complete that any alternative to care models that promise inclusion in mainstream community life has been shunned. Richard Grover (2007) wrote of intentional communities:

> But in so doing it has taken up a new certainty, that of living independently within the local community. Anything not reflecting this view tends to be regarded as part of the old order, therefore to be deplored. (Grover, 2007, p 3)

Just as opponents of the closure of institutions have been condemned as self-interested dinosaurs (Ingham, forthcoming), so discordant voices about the closure of community facilities are also dismissed as at best old-fashioned (Concannon, 2005). And yet, well over a quarter of a century after the discrediting of institutions, there is not a great deal of evidence that policies premised on community inclusion deliver a good-enough life for people. Emerson et al's (2005) survey indicates that 'community' has been idealised in the minds of policy makers (see

Chapter Nine), but that in reality communities are often unwelcoming and hostile. Metzel discusses the problematic nature of community for people who had lived in institutions: 'If we accept the premise that community is defined by social ties, meaningful interpersonal relationships, and belonging', she writes, 'then for people with mental retardation there have been two distinct communities' (2004, p 435).

For people who had lived in institutions, their community was the institution, and either it shifted as services moved, or it remained the institution where friends or work were located. For those who had never been institutionalised, then community was primarily their families, and the services that supported those families, including the parents' organisations. Ironically, she observes that community was inextricably linked to service systems, not what the ideology had intended. And, when those service systems are removed or diminished, as is happening as we write, then community disappears also.

Conclusion

This chapter has discussed the pendulum swings that characterise policy relating to intellectual disability. It has traced three phases over the past century. The institutionalisation phase used segregation to 'solve' the problem of mental deficiency as a source of social problems. It was intended to deliver a good or at least better life for the rest of society. This failed to provide an acceptable solution as families mobilised, and as costs continued to be high. Scandals about poor care resulted from institutions starved of funding and attention, as well as a flawed solution. The institutional solution was gradually replaced by a 'community care' solution, services that augmented both family and institutional care with a 'family-style' ethos. Intended to support families to achieve a better life, it created services that were buildings based, and provided day and residential 'care'. Costs did not decrease. At around the turn of the 21st century, 'community care' as a term began to fall into disuse. Influenced, we would argue, by the social model of disability, the challenge became to dismantle the barriers to people exercising citizenship rights, services needed to be personalised and individualised, buildings-based services would disappear as part of the discredited past, and a better life would follow. We are in the midst of this third phase.

The history of the past century indicates that intellectual disability has been, and continues to be, seen as a social problem. Faith has been placed in structural solutions to a perceived perennial social problem rather than focusing on what people might regard as a good life. Each successive phase is premised on discrediting the past and dismissing its solutions as misguided:'we now know better'. Yet there are constants. Families are constant, as is the desire to reduce costs, and, most importantly for our purpose, as are the views imposed by others with regard to how people should live. And the challenge of finding and nurturing a workforce to deliver these different solutions has been consistently underestimated and underfunded, an issue we return to in Part Three.

SIX

Changing constructions of work

'Paid work' does not explicitly feature in the exploration of the meaning of a good life in Chapter Two. However, it resonates through some of the themes that we identified. In Bauman's view of modern happiness, paid work is the means by which one can enter the pursuit of this elusive goal. The capacity to undertake paid work suggests an equality or citizenship that invites participation in the society and in the social contract that governs us. And paid work can be seen as one of the ways in which we exercise commitment and duty or virtue in our lives. It is also one means by which we might acquire wisdom, which shapes our view of a good life. It is one of the means that brings us into relationships with others.

Further as we will see in this chapter access to paid work currently enjoys a central place in thinking about how to enable people with intellectual disabilities to attain a better life, as this extract from *Valuing people now* (DH, 2009) illustrates:

> Good person-centred planning can take time. Rather than use this as an excuse for inaction, effective managers will already be planning to develop what we know people say is most important to them and what society expects for all other people – access to real, paid work. As well as providing income, paid work opens up other opportunities such as social networks ... reinvestment strategies should move from traditional day services to a social inclusion strategy. (DH, 2009, p 30)

It is for these reasons that we chose work as a case study with which to end Part Two.

Undoubtedly, many people with intellectual disabilities value work, particularly paid work. Marie talked a lot about work in her account. It is important to her. Many of the themes articulated in *Valuing people now* (DH, 2009) appear in her account. She recognises her obligation to earn money, and the self-esteem that comes with it:

> "You have to work for it really you know to get money, kind of thing. Everything can't be a piece of cake, like you

know. It was nice to work like you know. They were very good, like, you know. And I think I was the only person out of the whole lot that had a learning disability, I think so. It was good being the only one, like, you know."

She has been more successful in gaining paid work than many people with intellectual disabilities. Some of the work she did gave her companionship, a sense of belonging:

"I was in Failté house [community employment scheme] for two years. I was in reception. I got to know the other staff as people, you know. I got to know the person rather than what they looked like."

Even after leaving, some of this connection has remained:

"There's a lady who works at the office and she always is inviting me when they have parties, like the Christmas get-together, I'm always welcome at tea break, probably the only one who's invited. Sometimes I kind of think it would have been nice if I stayed there."

However, this sense of community was not a universal feature of her working life. In Scotty's she was 'nice to people', she got on with them, but did not see them out of work.

Jobs also gave a structure to her day, something to get up for, something to say when people asked her what she was doing:

"I was a year out of work doing nothing. A year. I slept a lot. It was hard, the year I was out like, it kinda felt like, like least now you know you get up for something, but before it was kinda, there was no boundary, it was kinda like you'd no life and Mum and Dad would ask 'What are you doing?' and when I went over to the centre sometimes to pay my rent they'd ask 'What are you doing?' People, everybody was asking 'What are you doing?' and why I wasn't at work, like. But it wasn't my fault, like."

But often there was not enough to do even when she had a job:

"I kind of did up to about 12.5 hours a week. I wished it had been more. I would have liked more. We asked but I

didn't get more.... I just [wanted] to be more busy. I was
told at the beginning it would be 12 and a half hours a week.
Sometimes [I only worked] for an hour a day. Sometimes
it was two hours. One week it was two days. There was no
point in them having me on when they didn't need me."

And then there was pay. Several of the jobs Marie did were unpaid.
Even when she was in work it was part time and did not offer sufficient
income to escape benefits:

"I went to the centre most days like. Doing tips and things.
Putting them into little, kind of boxes, and you put them
into little holes. We did it for companies or something. [I
didn't get paid for that.]

"And, then a couple of years after that, I think it was 98,
I started working in the garden centre next door [to the
group home]. I worked there kind of, but working in the
garden centre, wasn't what you'd call the ideal thing to be
doing. It was boring I thought. I remember watering plants
and things like that. I don't think I was really suited to
what they had, you know. Wasn't my piece of cake anyway.
I didn't get paid."

Finally, there was the nature of the work itself. The garden centre was
"boring", she was not suited to catering. In her words: "I think that
was the wrong job for me totally. I'm not domesticated".

Knowing what she really wanted to do was a problem:

"[No one asked me what I wanted to do.] I suppose I didn't
know myself. Really I didn't. You know they didn't come
and ask me 'Would you like to do this?' and you know sit
me down and [talk].

"They're [the employment service] looking for another
job for me. But see the last time I went to see her she said
'You don't really know what you want. You need to write
down on a piece of paper what you want and you don't
want'. She said 'You don't know what you want' and maybe
I don't know what I want. Maybe go back to college or
something. Not sure of that one really."

Marie chose to leave her job at Scotty's. She knew people might criticise
her for that. But just having a job was not enough:

"People probably think 'Oh you've got a job, that's fine,' but that isn't what I want really, you know. I think it's time to do something different, completely different, you know."

We will return to Marie's account at the end of this chapter.

Work in contemporary policy

The role of work in policy and practice deserves consideration because it illustrates well the power of changing ideological constructs around learning disability, and what constitutes a policy aim. As we write, access to work is a key policy goal.

The English revisiting of *Valuing people*, published in 2009, articulates the significance of work in giving people a social identity:

Work defines us: what will you be when you grow up? What do you do for a living? These are questions we all face from others when people want to get to know us. But they are questions seldom directed towards people with intellectual disabilities. (DH, 2009, para 3.43)

It goes on to state that the biggest challenge for the strategy to help people into paid employment is 'To help people, their carers and the staff and services that support them to believe work is a genuine possibility when they see few examples of it in practice' (para 3.45).

This is a prime example of the view that 'attitudes' are key to change. If people believe paid work is a possibility, then progress will be made. We can see here echoes of the People First statement, quoted in Chapter Four, that it is labels that get in the way of people getting what they want: their own home, relationships and paid jobs. The evidence that it is only attitudes that are at fault is flimsy. In the *Valuing people* strategy, evidence that people with complex needs can successfully hold paid jobs 'from some parts of both the USA and UK' is cited (para 3.46), although no examples are actually given.

The policy is about abandoning day services and using paid work as a vehicle for inclusion:

Stop thinking about 'day services modernisation' and instead work on people getting better lives in their communities by using person-centred planning, with access to work as the main starting point.

> Valuing People proposed day services modernisation in relation to services provided by adult social services departments. We now think that this term is unhelpful. It encourages people to think about buildings rather than outcomes. (DH, 2007b, pp 28–9)

Paid work permeates many of *Valuing people now*'s other 'Big Priorities' including 'personalisation'. Central to this issue is the goal of extending the use of person-centred planning (PCP) to enable work to play a central role in people's lives: 'Using outcomes from person-centred plans to design new opportunities and supports for people, with paid work at the centre of this' (DH, 2007b, p 7).

The policy proposes that the sort of work provided by services in buildings, such as Adult Training or Social Education Centres, the sort of work Marie did in Failté, should be replaced with a more flexible provision funded by direct payments and individual budgets. As more individuals' needs are assessed through PCP, their requirements will be met by their own personalised payments from local and national state benefits. The 'outcomes' will be that resources to meet these wants and needs will be found in the community at large, not in the local authority- or voluntary organisation-run building. The key outcome is accessing paid work.

We do not read much about the types of work people are expected to access, or how work may need to change if people are to access jobs in large numbers. It reads as a policy of insertion (Winance, 2007) in which the onus is on people and those who support them, rather than on rethinking work so that it can accommodate people with a wide range of abilities.

Work in the past

Work, and getting people labelled as having an intellectual disability to work, in fact has a very lengthy history, but not always couched in the positive terms of modern policy documents. Work by patients was a central feature of the old institutions. Robert McKenzie, resident in Lennox Castle Hospital, Scotland, from 1947–99 recalled:

> I had a lot of jobs. I used to help all the nurses every night. I got the laundry bags all ready for the wee ones to change at night. Tied the laundry and put it outside for the motors to take away. I shifted the coal in the boiler house, heavy work. Aye, I used to look after somebody as well. I used to

> take the wee boy out for a walk…. I'd feed all the wee ones
> that couldn't feed themselves. I used to help the ones that
> couldn't hold a spoon. (McKenzie, 2002, p 15)

Margaret Scally, another Lennox Castle resident (1968–90) said: 'You
used to all go down on your knees and do the scrubbing with short
night gowns and moleskins' (p 33).

Examples of work done by patients in institutions included:

> carpentry, book binding, envelope making, box making,
> tin smithing, tailoring, upholstering and mattress making,
> printing, needlework, painting, building, wood chopping
> and bundling, and shoe repairing. (Tizard and O'Connor,
> 1952, p 91)

There was considerable continuity in the types of work undertaken in
the day centres set up for the post hospital era in the 1960s and 1970s
(Carter, 1981). Humber cites the Greenwood Centre, an industrial
Adult Training Centre in Camden, London, which at its closure in
1993 was providing training in carpentry, printing, envelope making
and stuffing, box making and packing, and latterly laundry work
(Humber, forthcoming).

Work in institutions was a phenomenon across the world. From
Canada, 'Jinx' described how patients were required to 'line up and
mop floors in the morning' (Reaume, 2004, p 466) in an institution in
Ontario in the 1960s. Jinx received no payment for this work, though
when he left to become an outpatient labourer in 1973, he made picnic
tables and was paid $5.00 a week.

Work has had a variety of meanings in relation to people with
intellectual disabilities. Patients were an important source of labour,
essential to the working of institutions, to the extent that the discharge
of more able people in the 1950s threatened the economic viability
of institutional care, and may indeed have contributed to the decline
in standards that culminated in the scandals (Martin, 1984). Work was
cast as a privilege for high-grade patients, and it was valued by many,
despite being exploitative. 'Bert', for example, a 52 year old living in
a long-stay hospital, cast his biography in terms of the unpaid work
he had carried out there when I interviewed him in 1992 (Walmsley,
1995). The policy makers are probably more or less right in thinking
that work offers an important social identity. However, payment for

patient labour was minimal or non–existent. Pocket money payment, or payment in cigarettes or sweets, was common practice (Reaume, 2004).

Some residents of long–stay hospitals were allowed to work outside on licence (Atkinson, 1997b). The work was primarily on farms and in horticulture for men, and in domestic service, laundries and hotels for women (Atkinson, 1997b). Rolph speculates that work was used as an extension of the institution, in particular under the system of licensing some patients to work outside, as long as they were in positions where they could be kept under surveillance as live–in domestic labour, or in domestic roles in hospitals, nursing homes and so on (Rolph, 2000). This surveillance was particularly applicable to women patients whose ability to procreate was a matter of concern (Cox, 1996; Walmsley, 2000).

Work could also be regarded as punishment or even atonement – the endless scrubbing described by numerous ex–patients, male and female (see Atkinson, 1997a) – or more publicly acknowledged as therapy.

Farms, workshops and domestic labour in institutions, contract work carried out in training centres and sheltered workshops, all have elements of seeking to defray costs by putting people to manual labour. Work is good because it keeps people busy and enables people to pay off some of the costs of their care. Rex Blake Marsh, Medical Superintendant of Bromham Hospital, Bedford, argued that 'colonies' were an asset and 'can form a workshop wherein much useful work can be effected for the Local Authority' (Blake Marsh, 1943), just as Camden Council in London sent its laundry to the Greenwood Centre during the 1960s, rather than paying market rates (Humber, forthcoming).

Work was, however, most emphatically not about enabling people to live independent productive lives as consumer citizens, as it has become today (Dowse, 2009; Redley, 2009). Nor was it seen as an essential tool in the pursuit of modern happiness.

So, work has played a role in thinking and practice about managing the perceived problem that constitutes learning disability throughout the 20th century, through the twists and turns from institutional, to community care to personalisation. But as policy has changed, so has the meaning of work. From being a mechanism of control in the old institutions and the associated licensing system, to being a way to pass the time in the large centres characteristic of the care in the community era, to being the ultimate badge of inclusion now. What, we would argue, is constant, is that the work on offer has been manual and of low status, has never been fully remunerated at a market wage, has largely been carried out under close supervision, has most frequently been in special settings and, underlying this, has been seen as a means of defraying the costs of care, of ameliorating the 'burden' of economically unproductive members of society. Can we escape this through a new rhetoric of work as a badge of citizenship, a route to the good life, or is this simply old wine in new bottles?

Work: the ultimate badge of citizenship

The later 20th century saw work become reinvented as a badge of inclusion. No longer overtly about defraying costs, providing occupation, therapy or punishment, work was presented as a social good. As with much of the current policy agenda, this is supported by people with intellectual disabilities, the majority of whom, like Marie, do aspire to real jobs (Emerson et al, 2005). The reasons for this have been explored in Chapter Four, as part of the discussion on normalisation.

Paid work as an ideal goal has been adopted, somewhat uncritically, by many supporters of people with intellectual disabilities, including leading self-advocates, academics and advocacy organisations such as Mencap (England and Wales) (Redley, 2009). It is regarded as a good thing, an essential ingredient of a good life. One might regard this as enlightened, a route to full inclusion in society, and this is undoubtedly how it is intended to be read. However, it is work on society's terms, a classic instance of people being asked (and helped) to overcome the barriers that prevent their enjoying a conventionally defined 'good life', a policy of insertion rather than inclusion. Why has work come to enjoy this pre-eminent place as the key policy goal? Prideaux et al (2009, p 564) argue that this is because, 'Of late, work in the paid labour market, or at least actively seeking such work, is seen as the only means by which social inclusion can be fully achieved'.

Valuing people now, with its emphasis on paid work and the 'supply-side supports', such as job search, rehabilitation and financial inducements (Roulstone, 2000), represents a conceptualisation of the problem as being a failure of will, skill and imagination on the part of families, workers, agencies and employers. And yet, it is a paradox that what may define people with an intellectual disability is an inability to participate in the labour market as it operates currently on equal terms due to their impairment. This is reflected by a leading self-advocate:

> Business wants people who are numeric [sic] and literate. Fine, some people can do that but there are some people who are never going to be able to do that – what are we going to do? (Interview with the Chairperson of London People First, 19 May 1999, quoted in Dowse, 2009, p 571)

As Wilson demonstrated by reference to three individual examples, the 'supply-side supports' were not enough to counteract individual shortcomings, and practical difficulties: 'They were unable to compensate for Eve's illiteracy and general competence in particular areas' (2003, p 111).

Another interviewee quoted by Wilson, Sarah, could cope with many elements of her job in retail, but, despite support from her employer and a specialist training provider, ultimately failed to retain the job because she could neither pass the company induction course, nor travel unaided on public transport to help out when other stores were short-handed. Both were requirements of the job. Wilson concluded that success requires a rethinking of the nature of 'real jobs': 'The successful introduction of people with "learning difficulties" into the world of work requires a direct challenge to the construction of job descriptions' (2003, p 113).

Redley and Dowse have both, independently, analysed wider reasons within the paradigm of welfare ideologies and globalisation, respectively, for the emphasis on paid work. Dowse writes:

> The new technologies of welfare are economically driven and actively directed toward investing in the individual pursuit of independence, framing inclusion in terms of productivity and contribution, rather than self-fulfilment or quality of life. (Dowse, 2009, p 573)

Dowse considers this in terms of Beck's 'risk society'. The need to manage risk results in the stratification of people with intellectual disabilities, some are relegated to being non-productive burdens; while those deemed capable of managing risk with support, become subject to 'technologies of agency or of citizenship' and 'technologies of performance' (Dowse, 2009, p 577). Dowse writes:

> Technologies of agency or citizenship seek to enhance and improve the individual's capacities for participation and action ... 'at risk' groups are required to subject themselves to technologies of citizenship through which they agree to a range of normalizing therapeutic and training measures designed to empower them, enhance their self-esteem, optimise their skills and entrepreneurship and so on. (2009, p 577)

Preparation for participation in the labour market is an important way in which people are subject to these 'technologies'.

Technologies of performance are the complement to this (Dowse, 2009). These subject the work of agencies, such as supported employment agencies, to audit. She cites reforms to employment policy for people with disabilities in Australia, which count placements of individuals in supported or open employment settings as outcome measures. She argues that these reforms might enhance participation in the labour market, but that:

> they have also effectively removed the scope and capacity of employment services to perform the crucial work of community liaison and development that is so central to the creation of the supported and open employment opportunities upon which the service largely relies for its placements. (Dowse, 2009, p 579)

Seen in the light of this analysis, the better life promised via real jobs needs to be understood as an aspect of the reform of welfare, a reduction in the collectivity and an increasing individualisation of welfare provision.

Marcus Redley's analysis begins with an acknowledgment that despite welfare reform, which has resourced job-getting strategies by subsidies to employers, job coaching, job brokers and the like (Dowse's 'technologies of agency'), there is little evidence of success. He writes:

> People with learning disabilities are less likely to be employed and less likely to be economically active. Improvements in both the employment opportunities of adults with learning disabilities and their welfare have effectively stalled. (Redley, 2009, p 490)

He quotes Emerson et al's (2005) survey indicating earnings of less than £200 per week, with people opting for part-time work to protect income from benefits as the norm. Furthermore, Redley claims that the work is such that it provides little protection against social exclusion. It is low paid, low status and repetitive.

He, like the self-advocate quoted earlier in this chapter, would argue that the current emphasis on paid work is idealistic:

> To imagine that all adults with a learning disability could find paid employment on a par with their non-disabled

peers is to fall prey to a certain 'romanticism' (Burton and Kagan 2006) that obscures the obdurate nature of some disabilities (Abberley 2002; Shakespeare 2006) and the value employers put on particular skills and abilities. Many men and women with learning disabilities effectively inhabit a welfare enclave. They are either unemployed or unable to earn an income commensurate with that of their non-disabled peers. With this in mind, it is necessary to consider how welfare services might be further contributing to the social exclusion of citizens with learning disabilities. (Redley, 2009, p 493)

Redley's analysis points to the flaws in the idolisation of paid work as the pathway to a good life. Not only is it 'insufficiently rooted in economic reality' (2009, p 497), but, even when it is successful, it does not lead people to escape poverty or isolation. He concludes:

A model of citizenship, and hence of social inclusion, framed exclusively in terms of individual autonomy in employment and choices in public services is inappropriate for many men and women with learning disabilities, for it places insufficient value on the relational and convivial aspects of inclusion and participation. (2009, p 497)

Redley's language is very different to Marie's, but in this final sentence, they are saying very similar things – that work in itself does not provide the 'good life', rather it is companionship and relationships, intrinsic interest, and a sense of belonging and contribution that bring the benefits. Marie wanted to continue the advocacy work she was doing, unpaid:

"I would like to keep doing the work I am doing and keep doing what I am doing. As long as I can. And as long as I am helping somebody I am happy. As long as somebody gets something out of it I am happy, you know."

The low-paid and unskilled jobs that *some* people with intellectual disabilities are likely to obtain will not necessarily provide these. We pick up this relational theme in Part Three of the book.

Conclusion

This chapter has used the emphasis on paid work in current policy on intellectual disability to further consider how we have got to where we are today. Not only are people with intellectual disabilities unlikely to find work, but, when they do so, as Marie's story illustrates, it is almost invariably low paid, and lacks many of the benefits many people derive from work – interest, variety, companionship, social and geographical mobility, and enough money to purchase goods and services. The chapter has explored the way work has been socially constructed in different eras, and asks whether the contemporary fetish around work as a defence against social exclusion is justified. It has used Marie's story, and trenchant analyses by Dowse and Redley, to probe behind the shiny rhetoric, and question the centrality of paid work in current policy as a vehicle to deliver 'a good life'.

Part Three
Rethinking a good life

Introduction

In Part Three we seek to offer some alternative ways of thinking about a 'good life' for people with intellectual disabilities, and how we might move forward from the present impasse. We do so with some trepidation, knowing that better minds than ours have wrestled with such questions.

We begin, in Chapter Seven, by looking at a term that is widely used, but rarely unpacked: 'rights'. People's 'rights' are frequently cited, their operationalisation rarely explicated. We explore Martha Nussbaum's capabilities as an adjunct, to help think about what needs to be done if rights are to mean something in practice. In Chapter Eight, we take two more of the empty 'feel good' words with which policy is littered: community and inclusion. We ponder the paradox that at a time when geographical communities are the stuff of nostalgic dreams, people with intellectual disabilities are expected to be included in them. We offer in their stead 'belonging' as a goal, and explore where that takes us. Finally, in Chapter Nine, we look at the implications for the workforce, paid and unpaid. We deconstruct roles based on thinking about advocacy, and propose what workers paid and unpaid need to know and do if support is to move beyond 'tending'.

We do not claim to have found new solutions. Indeed, one of our criticisms as we reflect on how we arrived at today's prevailing ideology has been that blanket solutions are never going to be found. 'Solutions' are what policy makers crave, perhaps what we would all like, but the lurches we described in Chapter Five are not the answer as they create new doctrinaire prescriptions and rely on besmirching the unenlightened past. Thus have institutions been seen as the villain, rather than a symptom of a deeper challenge, just as institutional solutions had made villains of neglectful families; and just as segregated provision has been seen as the cause of continuing exclusion.

Our thoughts on alternative ways of thinking are grouped into three broad headings:

- Rights
- Communities and belonging
- Relationships

So far in this book we have reflected on how a 'good life' has been viewed in Western thought, and how these meanings of a 'good life' may apply to the situation of people with intellectual disabilities. In Part Two we explored the failure of policy and practice in relation to people with intellectual disabilities to really engage with what 'good life' might mean for this group of people. Chapter Five described three roughly sequential phases of reframing intellectual disabilities as a perceived continuing problem. Intellectual disabilities as a threat to society led to institutional solutions; intellectual disabilities as a threat to family life led to 'community care' solutions; and the denial of citizenship has led to policy solutions based on a discourse of individualism which reflects the current values in the wider society – a home, a paid job, choice and control. All have suffered from failures of implementation, and families have consistently been left as the mainstay for most people. For many, life remains nasty, poor and short. Much has changed, but much has remained the same.

We start Part Three with three propositions:

That there is a need to clarify what we mean when we develop policies in relation to the lives of people with intellectual disabilities. 'A good life' is not a new and better slogan, rather it provides a way of unpacking values and ideas which have a long history in Western thought and may help us to move beyond promoting a 'better life' for people with intellectual disabilities to an exploration of what a good life might mean. This means that we must face the facts that people with intellectual disabilities are not one group of people for whom the same life may be good. It also means that we need to confront the nature of the impairment that people may have and not treat all people as if they are the same

That the current way a 'good life' is conceptualised in policy may deliver important elements of a 'good life' for some, but by no means all, people with intellectual disabilities, and risks omitting key ingredients such as 'virtue', duty and commitment to others.

That 'inclusion' is a desirable goal, but that the way it is interpreted equates to 'insertion' into so-called normal life, and that we need alternative ways of thinking about inclusion if everyone is to have the ingredients of a 'good life'. Technologies of support – job coaches, personalised assistance, accessible information – will not take away the impairment that contributed to exclusion in the first place. In particular, we propose that a sense of belonging needs to be an explicit goal.

As we wrote this book we tried to consider alternative ways of conceptualising a good life, other than the main focus in our societies. Our work suggested the need for other ways of thinking about this issue. In other cultures a good life is conceived of differently. However we have come to the conclusion that attempting to fundamentally change the ways in which we currently conceptualise a good life are beyond our remit and capacity. So this third part of the book explores how we can make 'a good life' as conceptualised in our society work better for people with intellectual disabilities.

The catch phrases such as a 'life like any other' or an 'ordinary life' that have been used to herald changes in policy in our view do not help or guide us in finding ways to work with people with intellectual disabilities. They are empty labels which probably most of us would reject if applied to our own lives.

From our thought and reflection we believe that making a good life central to our work helps in a number of different ways:

- It is not an empty label but is a concept which has been thought about in different ways over a long period of time. It holds particular values which our society currently espouses, although of course does not always practice.
- It enables us to bring together the values which underpin a good life as it is conceived: freedom and constraint, the pursuit of happiness, the personal journeys we create. Not all of these things are necessarily valued equally and there is continuing debate about them in terms of their priority. But we see this debate as having the possibility of moving us forward.
- It places the individual firmly in the centre of the frame. In a good life we are not aiming for the least common denominator but for the very best ways that people can live.
- It provides us with some ways of evaluating and thinking about what a good life might be. And perhaps it opens up the debate and the engagement that might lead to different conceptions of a good life, not just for people with intellectual disabilities but for all of us.

SEVEN

Justice, rights and capabilities

This chapter is concerned with a central question: how far can the ideas embedded in contemporary views of rights and justice take us in the development of a good life for people with intellectual disabilities?

Rights

> Is there another word for rights. A lot of people (with intellectual disabilities) don't know what rights mean. (Roberts, 2009)

Like many other concepts addressed in this book, 'rights' is a generally used term, the meaning of which is seldom unpacked, and, as Bill Roberts says, for people with intellectual disabilities it can be a difficult one to explain in concrete terms. To describe the history and development of rights would take a book in itself, however we believe it is important to provide a brief account of how ideas about rights have evolved and their implications for people with intellectual disabilities. It is also important to position them in relation to the philosophical accounts in Part One of what constitutes a good life because:

> If we do not know what human rights are exactly, how they have developed and why they might be important, making a decision about how best they might be protected will be correspondingly more difficult. (Zifcak and King, 2009, p 11)

What are rights?

The conception of rights is deeply embedded in Western philosophical views about the nature of being human and of 'a life well lived' or, in our terms, 'a good life'. As we will see in this brief account, they resonate strongly with the discussion of a good life in earlier parts of this book.

Rights are not a new concept, although there has been a strong focus on them since the middle of the 20th century. They have their basis in theological writing and philosophy in the late middle ages.

Thomas Aquinas, for example, asserted that there were certain natural laws or principles of justice. He defined justice as 'what is owed to everyone in common' as opposed to obligations to particular individuals. Aquinas saw rights as entitlements that encompassed life, reason, determination of one's life course, peaceful living and the search for God. Enlightenment philosophers such as Kant and Mill removed rights from their theological context and reconstituted them as moral principles derived from reason alone.

The French and American Revolutions provided lists of rights that are the foundation of modern-day conceptions. And they also positioned them as claims on government in all its forms. They were the basis of political struggle and 'were to be fought for in the interests of justice' (Zifcak and King, 2009, p 12). They were fundamental in the development of both the Declaration of the Rights of Man, which followed the French Revolution, and the American Declaration of Independence.

The development of rights has always been based on what it means to be human and this, as we have seen in earlier chapters, is closely linked to the nature of a good life. In a recent discussion of human rights, Griffin (2007) argues that what makes us human is our ability to reflect and to act: 'our status as human depends on the capability we have to deliberate, assess, choose and act in ways that will advance our notion of a life well lived' (Zifcak and King, 2009, p 15). For Griffin human rights are needed to protect this construction of what it means to be human. He goes on to demonstrate how a failure to protect basic rights, for example to life, security of the person, political decision making, freedom to worship, assembly and a free press, injure us physically and psychologically, but more essentially injure our identity and dignity as human beings.

The UN Declaration of Human Rights is probably now the most well known of the statements of rights in modern times. It emerged from the horrors of the Second World War in the 20th century and sought to provide protection of rights that were closely allied to a recognition of what it meant to be human. The first three articles of the Declaration state:

- All human beings are born free and equal in dignity and rights. They are endowed with reason and conscience and should act towards one another in a spirit of brotherhood. (Article 1)

- Everyone is entitled to all the rights and freedoms set forth in this Declaration, without distinction of any kind, such as race, colour, sex, language, religion, political or other opinion, national or social origin, property, birth or other status. Furthermore, no distinction shall be made on the basis of the political, jurisdictional or international status of the country or territory to which a person belongs, whether it be independent, trust, non–self-governing or under any other limitation of sovereignty. (Article 2)

- Everyone has the right to life, liberty and security of person. (Article 3)

These rights are stated to be universal. However in the light of the earlier discussion of a good life, the emphasis on the centrality of reason to the nature of being human is significant. Disability is not explicitly covered in the list of groups included within the Declaration except in terms of 'other status'.

The Declaration was not the answer to rights for particular groups. Since its inception there have been many further actions taken by the UN to protect the rights of specific groups of people. These include women, children and, of key importance to us in this book, disabled people. Significantly all of these groups have at different times in the past been regarded as excluded from consideration in terms of a good life because of imputed flawed reason. In the next section we focus particularly on the rights of people with intellectual disabilities.

People with intellectual disabilities and rights: history

It has been repeatedly argued in the literature that historically people with intellectual disabilities were excluded from a consideration of their rights. Marginalised in the community or confined behind the walls of institutions, they were regarded as either a physical or genetic danger to the community or alternatively at risk from it (Wolfensberger et al, 1972; Johnson, 1998). The drive towards community living and the closure of large institutions from the middle of the 20th century was underpinned with a strong rights discourse, and one that owed much of its energy to the horrors of the Second World War and the rise of concerns about rights for other marginalised groups. In the USA the closure of many institutions occurred within a legal context of rights where it was argued successfully in the courts that institutionalisation was an infringement of the constitutional rights of people with intellectual disabilities (Rothman and Rothman, 1984). However, it is also fair to say that an economic discourse also framed deinstitutionalisation as there was an increasing recognition by governments that the decaying 19th-century institutions would require massive public expenditure to renovate or change (Johnson, 1998). Life in the community, it was argued, was both consistent with a societal focus on rights and was likely to be cheaper. The tension between the assertion of rights and economic constraints has remained and continues to be an issue of importance in considering a good life for people with intellectual disabilities.

The focus on rights led to a raft of anti-discrimination legislation in many Western countries, for example the Disability Discrimination Act 1992 in Australia, the Disability Discrimination Acts 1995 and 2005 in the UK, and the Americans with Disabilities Act 1990 in the US. While we would argue that such legislation is important, it has limited effectiveness because essentially it has sought to protect people with disabilities from discrimination on the basis of their impairments and has not positively asserted a set of rights that they hold. Second, in the USA and in other countries 'it has proved difficult to transform society's institutional structures and attitudes towards marginalised individuals' (National Council on Disability, 2008, p 6) and it has proved difficult for people with intellectual disabilities to seek redress when they do experience discrimination (Millear with Johnson, 2000).

At an international level there was also a growing recognition of rights of people with intellectual disabilities through a series of UN Declarations and other UN instruments. Even a cursory reading of these instruments reveals the changes in the way people with intellectual disabilities were perceived over the final 30 years of the 20th century. The Declaration on the Rights of Mentally Retarded Persons was passed by the General Assembly of the UN in 1971. The Declaration established that 'mentally retarded persons' have the same rights as other human beings. It specified rights to:

- Proper medical care, physical therapy, education, training, rehabilitation and guidance to develop their ability and maximum potential.
- Economic security and decent standards of living; to perform productive work and engage in any meaningful occupation.

- Life with their own families or foster care, and to participate in community life.
- A qualified guardian when required to protect their personal well-being and interest.
- Protection from exploitation, abuse, degrading treatment and to due process of law. (Enable, 2003)

It is significant to note in this Declaration, however, that rights to marry and have children were omitted from the final document (Owen et al, 2009, p 33).

This Declaration was followed in 1975 by the Declaration on the Rights of Disabled Persons, which affirmed the rights of people with disabilities as established in prior Declarations and also affirmed these without discrimination. It states:

> Disabled persons have the inherent right to respect for their human dignity. Disabled persons, whatever the origin, nature and seriousness of their handicaps and disabilities, have the same fundamental rights as their fellow-citizens of the same age, which implies first and foremost the right to enjoy a decent life, as normal and full as possible [to include, civil and political rights]. (Enable, 2003)

This Declaration firmly places disabled people in the position of 'citizens', a point we will come back to later, and also emphasises 'a decent life', which is defined as being 'normal' and as full as possible.

In 1982 the UN General Assembly adopted the World Programme of Action concerning disabled people, which stressed the equality of rights of all human beings. It placed disability within a context of social barriers and stressed the importance of disabled people having full participation:

> The World Programme of Action ... utilizes 'equalization of opportunities' as its guiding principle for the achievement of full participation of persons with disabilities, on the basis of equality, in all aspects of social and economic life and development. It moves from the strictly medical perspective, and adds to the 'social welfare' perspective the integration [of] the human rights dimension of persons with disabilities in all aspects of development. (Enable, 2003)

In 1993 the Standard Rules on the Equalization of Opportunities for Persons with Disabilities was passed by the UN. It provided guidelines for national action in three main areas: preconditions for equal participation, targets for equal participation and implementation measures.

However, in spite of these developments, internationally the human rights of people with disabilities remained largely unachieved as the following comment from Louise Arbour, UN Human Rights Commissioner, makes clear:

> The existing human rights system was meant to promote and protect the rights of persons with disabilities but the existing standards and mechanisms have in fact failed to provide adequate protection to the specific cases of persons with disabilities. It is clearly time for the UN to remedy this shortcoming. (quoted in Lecomte and Mercier, 2009, p 43)

UN Convention on the Rights of Persons with Disabilities

It is within this context that the UN Convention on the Rights of Persons with Disabilities was passed in 2006 and came into force with its 20th ratification in 2008. The process of developing the Convention was important as for the first time the drafting committee included disabled people. The Convention does not confer new rights but rather seeks to legally bind countries that ratify it to a set of international human rights through a regular reporting mechanism to an international committee. The Convention aims to establish mechanisms for both implementing and monitoring it in each country. It does not confer new rights on people, but aims to consolidate existing ones (Quinn, 2009).

While the committee was unable to agree on a definition of disability it states in Article 2 that:

> The purpose of the present Convention is to promote, protect and ensure the full and equal enjoyment of all human rights and fundamental freedoms by all persons with disabilities and to promote respect for their inherent dignity. Persons with disabilities include those who have long term physical, mental, intellectual or sensory impairments which in interaction with various barriers may hinder their full and effective participation in society on an equal footing with others. (UN Convention on the Rights of Persons with Disabilities, 2006)

The core values of the Convention as described in Article 3 are:

- Dignity.
- Individual autonomy (including the right to make one's own choices).
- Non-discrimination.
- Full and active participation and inclusion.
- Respect for difference.
- Equality of opportunity.
- Accessibility.
- Equality between men and women.
- Respect for the evolving capacities of children with disabilities.

The 50 articles of the Convention cover a broad range of rights, but have a strong emphasis throughout on 'inclusion' of people with disabilities within mainstream communities and on the removal of social barriers to full participation.

Rights and the good life for people with intellectual disabilities

The Convention has been seen as an important step forward by many disabled people. For example, submissions to the House of Lords and House of Commons Human Rights Joint Committee (2008) included the following points:

- The Convention puts the rights of disabled people on an equal footing with other people.
- It sends a message that the rights of disabled people are being taken seriously at both international and national levels.
- It is the first clear international statement that disabled people have the right to be 'treated as full and equal human beings'.
- It has the possibility of achieving a paradigm shift, which will enable people with disabilities to be seen as equal human beings with the full set of rights that that confers rather than as objects of charity and welfare.
- It establishes an international cross-cultural set of moral principles that apply to all people with disabilities.

More particularly, Gerard Quinn, who was involved in the drafting of the Convention, has stated that one of the key features of importance in the Convention is that:

> the Treaty basically places a mirror before society. It makes us face up to our own values – to our 'legacy values' of dignity, autonomy, equality and social solidarity. It forces us to acknowledge the large gap that still exists between the 'myth system' of our values and the 'operations system' of how these values are in fact dishonoured in daily practice. Thus the Treaty is a force for rationality as well as a vehicle for carrying these values squarely to the heart of the disabilities field. It contains an ethic of justification that requires States to respond. (Quinn, 2009, p 246)

The implications of rights for people with intellectual disabilities

There are some important implications for people with intellectual disabilities in the discourse around rights:

- They have been seen as a means of conferring recognition of full citizenship and personhood on this group of people and, in line with some of the ideas in the social model of disability, they place the responsibility for achieving justice for this group on government and on the society.
- The rights discourse owes much to Western philosophical accounts of what it means to be a person including, as noted in Article 1 of the UN Convention, a focus on 'reason', reflection and conscience. As discussed earlier in this book, such a focus relegates those whose reason is perceived to be flawed to a marginalised position where they are seen as objects of charity rather than included as full citizens (Nussbaum, 2000).
- If the UN Declaration is in fact, universal, the question arises as to why specific Declarations and Conventions have been seen to be necessary for specific groups. It is perhaps significant that many of these groups have been those who historically have been seen to have less equality in terms of reason (for example women and children) and who have therefore been more prone to oppressive practices.
- The Convention on Rights for Persons with Disabilities was deemed necessary because previous actions by the UN were seen to be unsuccessful in achieving justice or protecting the rights of this marginalised group. Because the Convention entails legal accountability by states for their actions if they ratify it, it is hoped that this will lead the Convention to be stronger in achieving its ends.
- It is clear from the failure of previous attempts to safeguard the rights of disabled people effectively that the words of the Convention

need to be translated into actions and it is here that there are major problems. Not only do national and international rights statements require action by governments, but they also depend on how organisations and community members see the groups they address. Rights instruments can ensure that doors are forced open in the community for particular groups, but they cannot, however, shape the practices that happen once people enter those doors.

- International rights instruments are formed on the basis of discussion and compromise and although the new UN Convention on the Rights of Persons with Disabilities is unique in that it included disabled people in its development, its wording remains generalised and the means of achieving principles such as 'respect for difference' are not spelled out.
- The Convention in particular is very much within the current thinking about disability in Western societies in its emphasis on independence, choice, inclusion and control. These issues are important; however, they again leave groups of people marginalised for whom these issues may not be achievable (even when all obstacles are removed).
- Finally and most importantly for our discussion, in our view, rights set a minimum framework that has to be established and maintained by the society in which people with intellectual disabilities live. The Convention offers some hope that through states' accountability paper rights may be more readily translated into practical effects on people's lives.

These provide the foundation for building a good life, but do not equate with it. The importance of a consideration of individual values and desires, the need for the individual to be an active agent in creating their own good life, cannot be legislated for by the Convention. We need something more.

Capabilities and justice

The capabilities approach developed by Sen (1992) and in a more philosophical form by Nussbaum (2000, 2001b, 2006) is of central importance to this book as it draws on 'Aristotle's ethics on the purpose of a humanity being to realise "a good life"' (Carpenter, 2009, p 357). Central to Nussbaum's approach to capabilities is a conception of the dignity of the human being and consequently of a life that is worthy of such dignity, a life that she sees as having 'available in it truly human functioning' (Nussbaum, 2006, p 74). Such a life demands a consideration of all human activities and involves 'opportunities for action, not simply quantities of resources' (Nussbaum, 2006, p 75). While both Sen and Nussbaum have developed a capabilities approach, in this chapter we are concerned primarily with Nussbaum's account of capabilities as she has focused particularly on the place of disabled people in our society (Nussbaum, 2006). The capabilities approach that she enunciates is integrally related to a consideration of social justice issues. Nussbaum provides a critique of current theories of social justice with a particular focus on John Rawls. In particular, she notes that disabled people are explicitly excluded from his theory of justice. She expounds a version of rights that is premised on the dignity of human beings and respect for them, whoever they may be and in whatever culture they may live, and sees this approach as including disabled people as full members of the society.

She is not arguing that a capabilities approach is equivalent to 'a good life', but rather that it provides a basic social minimum that will enable human beings to flourish (Carpenter, 2009). However, her account of capabilities in our view takes us beyond the human rights as specified in the UN Convention for reasons that we will discuss later in this chapter.

What are capabilities?

Capabilities are those things that 'people are actually able to do and to be, in a way that is informed by an intuitive idea of a life that is worthy of the dignity of a human being' (Nussbaum, 2006, p 70). Nussbaum proposes a list of 10 central human capabilities that she sees as minimum social entitlements. She does not propose that these are exhaustive, and they are subject to change. The 10 capabilities that she sees as central are:

1. Life: not dying prematurely and being able to live fully to the natural end of one's life.
2. Bodily health, which includes adequate nourishment and shelter as well as being able to have good health.
3. Bodily integrity, which includes freedom of movement, freedom from violence and having opportunities for sexual satisfaction and choice in relation to having children.
4. Senses, imagination and thought. This includes being able to use these in ways that are 'truly human' and which may include the creation of artistic literary, religious or scientific works. Integral to this is the provision of education, which should not only focus on

literacy and numeracy. This capability includes freedom of expression and the experience of pleasure and the avoidance of pain.

5. Emotions, which includes being able to love and care for others and to experience that in return, 'to love, to grieve, to experience longing, gratitude, and justified anger' (Nussbaum, 2006, p 77). This demands that these emotions are recognised in the individual and also that support is given to human associations that foster them.

6. Practical reason forming a conception of what is good and planning and reflecting on one's own life. Support needs to be given to this through freedom of conscience and religious expression.

7. Affiliation. Nussbaum differentiates two kinds of affiliation. The first refers to our being able to live and feel with others and the second is concerned with the respect and dignity owed to the individual by others.

8. Other species is concerned with our living with concern for the world of nature.

9. Play, 'being able to laugh, to play, to enjoy recreational activities' (Nussbaum, 2006, p 77).

10. Control over one's environment. This capability is divided into two parts. The first is concerned with participation in political decisions that are relevant to one's life and protection of free speech and association. The second part is concerned with rights to hold property and to seek employment equally with others and to form associations with other workers (from Nussbaum, 2006, pp 76–8).

The relevance of capabilities to a good life for people with intellectual disabilities

The capabilities approach, we believe, offers a different perspective to considering the rights of disabled people in our society for the following reasons.

Placing the individual as central

The capabilities approach identifies human beings as an end in themselves and a good life as premised on the responsibility of states and communities to provide relevant supports for people to live dignified and full lives. While it may not offer a prescription for a good life, it does provide a holistic foundation for one. Further, although it does not explicitly state this, the assumption on which it rests is that the individual is an active agent in their own lives. So the way in which the capabilities are worded is in terms of the activity of the individual. Rather than 'being included' in society or the 'community' the individual is supported to create a life with choices and to develop their own life narratives.

Taking the subjective world into account

As noted in earlier parts of this book, we believe that one of the difficulties people with intellectual disabilities experience in living 'a good life' is the failure to take into account their internal worlds or subjective being. From Marie's story came the view that her life yearnings and dreams were not easily heard by others. While the new UN Convention places a strong emphasis on inclusion and participation, it does not take account of the dreams and desires of the individual. One of the issues that excited us about the capabilities approach as stated by Nussbaum was the focus on a variety of internal subjective experiences as part of the set of capabilities. While she (like other philosophers discussed earlier in this book) gives some emphasis to reason, reflection and life planning in her account, she also focuses on other, often ignored themes that are central to our lives. In terms of a good life, we noted earlier in this book that feelings, imagination and passion have been given short shrift in many philosophical accounts of a good life. The capabilities approach offers the potential for a rich and comprehensive set of minimum requirements for what a good life might mean for and by an individual.

Capabilities and social justice

The capabilities approach is integrally related to a consideration of social justice. However, it is a view of social justice that goes beyond a consideration of distributive justice. Indeed Nussbaum argues that a focus on economic and utilitarian measures of 'quality of life' is insufficient for a number of reasons. A reliance on income measures does not take into account the differences between people in terms of their economic needs. So, for example, a disabled person may need a higher income than a non-disabled person because of the costs associated with their impairment. Income measures do not allow for this kind of difference. She also criticises utilitarian measures of satisfaction with life because they do not take into account the previous experiences of people, which may lead to lowered expectations of satisfaction. This resonates strongly with earlier discussions of the lives of people with intellectual disabilities who may have experienced institutionalisation or negative life experiences leading to low expectations of what is possible. So, for example, Marie sees her independence in a flat of her own as a positive part of her life, but is unable to do more than dream wistfully of adult intimacy or relationships. Nor is the lowered expectation only felt by some people with intellectual disabilities. We believe that it is encapsulated in the policy emphasis on a 'better life' for people with intellectual disabilities with its focus on comparing their lives with the past rather than considering them in relation to other citizens' choices (Tøssebro, 2005).

Capabilities as a guide for planning and practice

One of the reasons that we were excited by the capabilities approach was its potential for working *with* people with intellectual disabilities. Thinking about capabilities takes us beyond much of the practice associated with person-centred care or individualised planning because it moves beyond the material goods and services that are so frequently the focus, and into more spiritual and emotional realms. Play, emotion, imagination and the senses are not terms that are often used in considering the lives of people with intellectual disabilities. A capabilities approach can extend practice into this important realm.

What would it mean if service providers or personal assistants took the 10 capabilities outlined by Nussbaum as central in their work. In our view it would mean that they would have to take account of the particular characteristics, desires and needs of the individuals with whom they were working. A consideration of how to support an individual in 'play', for example, would require a consideration of what this means to the individual and how they may want to exercise this. Returning to Marie's story, she provides an account of how she would like opportunities to engage in 'play' or recreational activities of dancing and socialising, but wants support to do this. She is quite clear in her need for someone of the same age who would be willing and interested in going with her to clubs and pubs. While she has a support person who is also a friend, Marie is well aware that this person is of a different age and has different interests to her. Working with Marie to explore how she might engage with younger people and express herself in activities that she sees as important in her life would then become a part of the work of those around her. While this may be seen as a role by some personal assistants or service providers, it is clear from the account of the current workforce that this kind of activity is not given a high priority. Using Nussbaum's capabilities as a guide to work with people with intellectual disabilities provides a basis from which to begin discussions and develop strategies with someone that may provide the foundation for a good life.

It could be argued that the capabilities approach is a retreat to a focus on the individual rather than a movement for social change. However, it is clear that in the planning and support for people to exercise capabilities there is a need to address the degree to which the community and society provide these opportunities or prevent them from being realised. This necessitates the involvement of disabled people themselves, but also those working with and advocating for them to become involved collectively in removing barriers that may prevent them from leading 'good lives' (Burchardt, 2004).

Capabilities and policy

Earlier discussions in Part Two of this book have focused on the way in which policy in relation to people with intellectual disabilities has tended to project on to them dominant values from the wider society without due regard to the nature of the life to which this may lead. We have also noted that in part this has been a consequence of constituting people with intellectual disabilities as a problem, either to the society in which they live, to their families or in relation to their inclusion in society.

The capabilities approach offers the opportunity to move beyond the ideological and societal imposition of a particular way of life and to consider what a good life might mean for individuals with different desires and also with different levels of impairment. A consideration of what work might mean, for example, for Marie who has particular commitments and interests and what it might mean for someone who is unable to articulate their position and is unlikely to engage in paid work may remove some of the 'stuckness' that we have noted in relation to policies and practices. The capabilities approach, if taken seriously, would allow for the same kind of diversity in life narratives that others in society create rather than imposing one particular way of life on a whole group of citizens.

Capabilities and the good life

There are strong resonances in the capabilities approach with the discussion of a good life in earlier parts of this book. This is hardly surprising since Nussbaum's list has been derived:

through a combination of philosophical enquiry, examination of religious, literary and utopian texts across cultures and ages and interaction with contemporary groups of poor and deprived people in the USA and in India. (Burchardt, 2004, p 743)

Like many philosophers of a good life, Nussbaum places practical reason, reflection and life planning as one of the capabilities. As Burchardt (2004) notes, and as we have also discussed, this poses a possible problem in relation to people with intellectual disabilities. Are they yet again precluded from living a good life? We take heart from the inclusion of other subjective qualities that are included in Nussbaum's list and also from the view that she expounds (Nussbaum, 2006) that we need to be creative in working with people with intellectual disabilities in relation to supporting them. She also makes clear that while her list has evolved to its current state, it is not a prescription, but rather a starting point for discussion and re-evaluation by groups of citizens. The degree to which a capacity is exercised may vary with the individual, but the support for it to be exercised is a responsibility of the community or society.

Nussbaum does not include contentment or happiness as part of her capabilities list for good reason. She argues that a good life is not necessarily one in which an emphasis is given to these issues. After all, one may choose to engage in activities that are frustrating and that are not accompanied by happiness, but which are fulfilling and can be seen as part of a flourishing life, for example writing books or engaging in artistic endeavours.

Conclusion

Neither the UN Convention on the Rights of Persons with Disabilities nor the capabilities approach provide people with a good life. In our view they are complementary instruments that can be used in practice to create the foundation for a good life. This demands a knowledge of what they may mean by people with intellectual disabilities and a commitment to achieving them by people who work with and advocate for them.

EIGHT

Community, inclusion and belonging

This chapter addresses the questions:

- What are the implications of the ideas about a good life for the lives of people with intellectual disabilities?
- What values relevant to defining a good life underpin current disability theories, ideas and discourses?
- What contribution have these values made to the lives of people with intellectual disabilities?

One of the strands of a good life identified in Chapter Two is that it is a life that balances virtue with pleasure, and duty with commitment; where human needs for work/purposeful activity and love/meaningful relationships are fulfilled. Fundamentally, it is a life lived with and for others. How are these to be achieved by and for people with intellectual disabilities? Faith has been placed in two concepts, 'community' and 'inclusion'. In this chapter we review these as mechanisms for achieving a better life, and find them wanting. We propose instead that 'belonging' and relationship-building may offer more tangible ideas to inform the journey to a good life.

The dream of community

> One of my hopes is that you and I and people everywhere will be able to build communities based on trust, places more like villages, where neighbours have names and faces, where their concerns gradually become our concerns. My dream is a society that becomes more deeply human, more hopeful. (O'Connor, 2008)

In the context of economic crises Cardinal O'Connor addresses what he sees as a breakdown in 'community'. His advocacy for a new approach is based on a view that has been advanced by a number of theorists (Lasch, 1995; Bauman, 2001) that we have lost something that we should value, a sense of connection with each other. Essentially the

Cardinal advances a nostalgic view of community that seems to be based on geographical proximity. It reminds us of an idealised world that is now largely seen in sitcoms or 19th-century novels where neighbours knew each other and were intimately involved with each other's lives. Perhaps it is the setting for the 'ordinary life', or a life like any other (Chapter Four).

It is ironic that at a time when geographical communities are in decline, the stuff of nostalgia, people with intellectual disabilities are expected to find a life like any other in 'community'. Harking back to the past does not help. Any perception that in the past communities included people with intellectual disabilities and their families is challenged by the historical record. Mr and Mrs York, a Jewish couple who lived in East London all their lives, had no friends themselves, and nor did their son:

> Ben has never had friends. Never gone to other people's houses. We would like him to branch out... but he can't use the buses because he doesn't recognize the bus numbers.
> (Mr and Mrs York, 2005, p 166)

Mr and Mrs York were in their 80s when this interview was conducted in 2001. Theirs had been a lonely lifetime vigil with and for Ben. They recognised the value of friends, to Ben, and also to themselves, but they did not know how to find and keep friends. And no one ever helped them. Instead 'they' 'cut' the service that took Ben out at weekends and in the evenings, and left this couple saying 'We would like more respite now we are older' (p 166). In mid-20th-century rural Ireland, contrasting sharply with urban inner London, Patrick Kearney describes his (integrated) village school as 'brutal', for all, and particularly for himself (Kearney with Johnson, 2009, p 25).

Two stories can only tell us so much. Maybe the Yorks were unlucky. Maybe Patrick's experience in his village school was exceptional. But variants of these stories of exclusion are told in different ways by too many people (Bornat, 1997). The challenge is not to recreate a nostalgic past, which may never have existed in reality. Rather it is to forge deeper understandings of the barriers people have confronted in living in the community, what we actually mean when we glibly talk of inclusion, and to allow ourselves to think differently about ways to build relationships. Part of this challenge is to acknowledge some of the contradictions in current thinking about inclusion and about community.

Inclusion, community and people with intellectual disabilities

Inclusion has been conceptualised as:

> A powerful philosophical tool, as it implies both the possibility for, and the right of, people with disabilities to experience life fully among the people and places in their environment. It is sometimes used in the sense that society has an obligation to accept and accommodate every one of its members, including all people with disabilities. (Brown and Brown, 2003, p 6)

Brown and Brown's definition is relatively straightforward. However, in practice the meanings of inclusion for people with intellectual disabilities have changed over time. Three broad understandings of inclusion have emerged since the 1970s.

In the 1980s inclusion was about people not being physically apart from the community by living in institutions (Brown and Brown, 2003). 'Community' became seen as the antithesis to institutions (Johnson, 1998; Johnson and Traustadottir, 2005). This first phase was associated with integration. Segregation was seen as 'bad' both because of the conditions in which people were forced to live, leaving them open to abuse and to poor-quality lives and because it was wrong in principle to isolate people from community life. People with intellectual disabilities were encouraged not to have friends who had disabilities (Chappell, 1997) and not to regard staff as friends. They were encouraged to wear age-appropriate clothing, and, in the notorious 'conservative corollary', to wear formal clothing even beyond the requirements of the context in which they found themselves, to diminish the risk of devaluation This was based on the view that exclusion of people with intellectual disabilities had to do with them having 'devalued characteristics'. Shaping of behaviour was required, alongside structural and legislative changes in order that people may be accepted into 'normal' communities' (Wolfensberger, 1975).

The second phase saw ideas about inclusion focused on how individuals' needs and interests could be taken into account as they lived in the community. This has been given meaning in practices such as person-centred planning and its variants (Brewster and Ramcharan, 2005). Influenced by the social model of disability (Oliver and Barnes, 1998) there was a shift to regarding the structures and processes of society as disabling. Inclusion was reconceptualised as involving social change as well as change to the individual.

Most recently, in a third phase, the importance of personal relationships and emotional well-being (Arthur, 2003) has been articulated in discussion about the meaning of inclusion. Rights and citizenship are argued to be necessary prerequisites, but not sufficient, for the development of meaningful relationships between people. Similarly, having varied and valued social roles sets the scene for varied social relationships, but does not ensure friendship and belonging (McConkey and Collins, 2009). This point is made by Reinders (2002, p 23): 'A good life for human beings is shared with friends – a life that can only thrive in a properly arranged and regulated public space'.

A more structural approach to the issues affecting inclusion in community, not only by people with intellectual disabilities, has been the promotion of programmes that seek to develop social capital. Social capital involves a focus on the strengthening of relationships within (bonding) and between (bridging) communities, building trust, community strength and self reliance (Winter, 2000).

These rather different meanings of inclusion coexist in current policy. The English Social Care Institute for Excellence defined the 'good life' as: 'doing things which have a purpose and are meaningful for the individual'; 'doing things in ordinary places, that most members of the community would be doing'; 'doing things uniquely right for the individual'; and 'meeting local people and developing a sense of belonging' (SCIE, 2008, p 8).

This combines a personalised view of inclusion, things that are 'uniquely right for the individual' (Phase 2), an emphasis on relationships and belonging (Phase 3), alongside a remnant of the original emphasis on 'ordinary places', an echo of the 'ordinary life' of the 1980s.

Inclusion is a widely used and poorly defined concept that has come to mean different things to different people. This is in common with other terms adopted within disability ideology and policy, such as rights and independence, which have been described as 'conceptually confused' and forming a poor basis for research (Rapley, 2003b).

Community

Initially ideas about 'community' were framed as if it offered the ideal alternative to institutional living. There was a homogeneous idealistic approach to the understanding of 'community', a failure to recognise its diversity and complexity (Bauman, 2001). The mechanisms by which inclusion into the community of ordinary people (whatever that is) is expected to occur rely more on structural change – closure of 'special' segregated settings, 'mainstreaming' education and health care, anti-discrimination legislation – than they do on relationships and the means by which social capital is created.

'The community' can be a hostile place. At the time of writing (October 2009), the death of Fiona Pilkington and her 18-year-old daughter who had an intellectual disability hit the headlines. Fiona lived with her daughter 'in the community'. She set fire to herself and her daughter, apparently in despair that no one had heard her pleas for relief from harassment at the hands of local youth (Walker, 2009, p 1). There is risk in not tackling the realities of life in the community to which people with intellectual disabilities are particularly vulnerable, such as abuse, exploitation, poverty and isolation (Ticoll, 1994; Bates and Davis, 2004). Failure to respond to these issues can mean neglect, loneliness or worse, and can create fertile ground for segregation to resurface despite all the known disadvantages.

There has been only limited recognition of the point made by Metzel (2004) and quoted in Chapter Five that, historically, community has been inextricably linked to service systems. However regrettable, community (meaning social ties, meaningful relationships and belonging), for most people with intellectual disabilities, has been framed either by relationships developed through segregated service provision, or by families and their networks, and the services that support them. Robertson et al (2001) researched the social networks of 300 people with intellectual disabilities, and found that the average social network was between three and eight people, and these consisted primarily of staff, a family member and another person with an intellectual disability. When segregated provision goes, there is a danger that the limited social ties, relationships and belonging that they offer also disappear.

We are not saying that social networks defined by intellectual disability are what we should aim for. But we are beginning to think that to discard them as part of a discredited past may be a mistake, and that building on them may have more value.

Inclusion in broader thinking

Ideas about inclusion in intellectual disability can be compared to more ambitious ideas about inclusion proposed in the context of the broader society:

- Active and acknowledged citizenship within a particular society (Rose, 2000).

- Participation in decision making that affects one's own life and those of others with whom one is linked (Young, 2000).
- Access to resources and privileges within the society in which one lives (Rose, 2000).
- Opportunities to develop relationships with others with whom one shares common interests and characteristics and with those from whom one is different (Putnam, 2000).
- Opportunities to participate in shaping the way a society is developing (Cox, 1996).

One can see the pedigree of these ideas in the debates about a good life discussed in Chapter Two. The included citizen is premised on the ideal of an autonomous rational being. Consequently, the realisation for people with intellectual disabilities is problematic. Despite bold policy statements, their citizenship is compromised, as we showed in Chapter Seven. They lack access to resources and privileges (Emerson et al, 2005). Opportunities to develop relationships are limited due to lack of mobility, jobs, internet access and the like, not to mention wider societal attitudes (Seale and Nind, 2009). And, except in exceptional circumstances, such as policy consultations, there is precious little opportunity to shape the way society develops (Redley and Weinberg, 2007). We would argue that thinking about inclusion and community has failed to take account of the underpinning assumptions that fundamentally exclude.

This points to a contradiction at the heart of inclusion, that it is always a work in progress, never achieved. Inclusion requires difference to give it meaning. Inclusion is a one-way process – people with intellectual disabilities must travel into the communities of ordinary life, populated by non-disabled people. No one travels the other way. Clapton argues that inclusion is premised on a fixed concept of 'normalcy' to which excluded people can, by definition, never belong. She writes:

> This is because inclusion is at one with a dichotomy – exclusion – based upon an assertion that there is a normal to which socially excluded people aspire, but of which they can never truly be members because that would undermine the dichotomy. (Clapton, 2009, p 204)

In Chapter Four we traced this back to ideals associated with normalisation. Despite challenges to the concept of 'normal' by disabled academics (French, 2004), the premise posed by Goffman has remained as a fundamental underpinning assumption – there are disabled and non-disabled people. However successful people are in 'passing' as normal, or becoming accepted into the mainstream, they remain stigmatised and disabled. Inclusion can never happen if this is the way disability is viewed.

Myriam Winance (2007) offers an alternative way of thinking about relationships between disabled and non-disabled people. Drawing on Garfinkel's ethnomethodology, she argues that norms are negotiated within social interactions, rather than being external to the actors. In other words, Winance proposes that the stigma and disadvantage associated with disability is not the product of a Goffmanesque clash between the stigmatised and the 'normals', in which the normals set the rules and the stigmatised do their best to negotiate them. Rather these issues are mediated within social relationships. Things can be managed between people as they work to produce a new or different social order where normal is under constant negotiation between social actors. What society means is not known, not a given, rather it is created and recreated in social interaction.

The idea that a 'good life' for people with intellectual disabilities is premised on relationships is not new. Even Edgerton, arch exponent of the idea that the task of 'retards' was to manage their 'stigma', found that people who could rely on a 'benefactor' were more successful in negotiating life on the outside.

Thinking in this way opens up infinite possibilities for community and belonging that move away from the one-way traffic assumed in much policy and literature.

Belonging

What happens if we replace 'community' and 'inclusion' with 'belonging' as a goal? The importance of belonging has been captured by bell hooks (2009) who quotes Loyal Jones in her preface to a set of essays on the subject:

> We think in terms of persons, we remember the people with whom we are familiar and we have less interest in abstractions, and people we have only heard about. (Loyal Jones, quoted in hooks, 2009, p 4)

Abstractions characterise thinking and writing about inclusion and community. Belonging, because it is built on place, memory and relationships, can be more concrete. hooks reminds us that at the core of 'community' are people, the people who matter to us. She proposes that memory is central to a sense of belonging:

> We are born and have our being in a place of memory. We chart our lives by everything we remember from the mundane moment to the majestic. We know ourselves through the art and act of remembering. (hooks, 2009, p 4)

Belonging, unlike inclusion, implies a past as well as a present. Unlike, perhaps, the exercise of reason, people with intellectual disabilities are not excluded by the lack of memory, or lack of a past. But they are, through force of circumstance, highly vulnerable to loss through frequent and often forced moves (Beadle-Brown et al, 2005); through a lack of care on their behalf about possessions and artefacts that support memory; and, argues Jayne Clapton (2009), through a reluctance by some of us to listen.

Supporting memory

Clapton argues that 'to be a person is to have a story' (2009, p 241), and that when stories remain silent 'personhood is diminished' (p 241). Everyone has a story; but some stories are not told, heard or recorded. In the lurches of policy described in Chapter Five, individuals are told to forget their past, and to move on into a better present. This view translates into practice in dramatic ways. Sheena Rolph describes being present when staff tore up the scrapbooks former residents of Little Plumstead Hospital brought to their new hostel (Rolph, personal communication). The message is that the belonging they represent is now meaningless, to be consigned to the dustbin.

Life story work can recover this sense of life as a journey. It allows people to represent themselves as complex human beings, with an identity, rather than being defined by their label as part of a homogeneous group whose characteristics are recorded only in case files (Atkinson, 2005). Mabel Cooper, who published her life story, described its importance thus:

> I think it was nice for me to be able to do something, so that I could say 'I've done it.' It made me feel that it was something I had done. You've got something so that you can say, 'This is what happened to me.' Some of it hurts, some of it's sad, some of it I'd like to remember. My story means a lot to me because I can say, 'This is what happened to me,'

> if anyone asks. So it's great, and I will keep it for the rest of my life. I will keep the book. (Atkinson et al, 1997, pp 9, 11)

Life stories allow for people to own a difficult past, to move from silent victims to active representation of their lives (Rolph and Atkinson, forthcoming). Constructing life stories is an instance of co-production, people with and without disabilities working together to produce something of lasting value, not only to themselves, but to others.

Most life story work has been with people with relatively mild disabilities (Booth and Booth, 1996; Cooper, 1997). Sue Ledger has shown the value of imaginative methods in recording life stories with people with higher support needs. She used mobile interviews, in which she drove around with people labelled as having challenging behaviour or complex needs to revisit places of significance for them. She describes the subtle interaction of people with community as place in this extract:

> PB had not been back to his former family home for at least 10 years yet he knew it immediately. Watching PB standing outside the entrance to the family maisonette he had shared with his mum and three brothers I could really picture him as a child with his older brothers.... Through accompanying Paul and seeing his familiarity and enthusiasm for the area where he had spent his childhood, I felt I gained a much greater understanding of the significance of his former home to him and of what a change it had been for him to move from a close happy family to sharing with relative strangers at the hostel. (Ledger, forthcoming)

Perhaps most significant was the use of the Life Maps created through this detailed research. One participant commented on their importance as a way of sequencing his life story in one place, counteracting the 'problems with time' referred to by Booth and Booth (1996):

> RE: Before it was like in bits. I think some of it was in the old files and things. I couldn't remember it in my head. Now it's here in front of me and I can show people where I was born and tell it all from there. If I forget anything I just look at the photographs. (Ledger, forthcoming)

The maps were used to allow people to be known, with their histories, to staff:

AL said that before putting together her life book and accompanying life map staff in her support team had not known about the 27 years she had spent in Normansfield hospital.

'I showed them the photograph of the hospital ... here [points to picture of former long-stay hospital on her life map]. M [member of staff] didn't believe me ... she said you weren't in hospital you lived with your family.' (Ledger, forthcoming)

The maps gave staff, most of whom lived at a distance, a sense of the place where they worked as having meaning for the people they work with and for, and pointed to hitherto unsuspected commonalities of experience, such as losing a parent at a young age, or growing up on a council estate. Ledger's research gives meaning to the idea of community as memory, as relationships, and points to the potential of Winance's argument that:

One does not integrate disabled people into society, one simultaneously builds the normal person and the collective in which he/she will be included. And this work on the norm transforms everyone (with or without impairments) involved. (Winance, 2007, p 634)

Life story work points to ways in which this transformation can be fostered if we place 'belonging', rather than inclusion or community, at the centre of attention.

Family

The emphasis in policies of inclusion has been on the rights of adults with intellectual disabilities to live fulfilling lives in their own right, escaping from reliance on families (Rolph et al, 2005). But we know that in practice most adults in most developed countries continue to rely on families, if not for care, then for companionship, guidance and ongoing stewardship (Barron and Kelly, 2006; Hatton, 2008). Families are, for better or worse, at the heart of belonging. Not only because families provide a continuing link to our history but because it is in families of origin that we first formulate our sense of how we relate with others, where we belong, and this can inform the rest of our lives. In the twists and turns of policy, families have been regarded as the mainstay of care (Walmsley, 2006), the victims of almost intolerable burdens (see, for example, Ayer and Alaszewski, 1984) and have also been regarded as the barriers to people living a good life by being overprotective, interfering or infantilising (Rolph et al, 2005).

The family as a resource for building relationships has been little explored. Ramcharan and Grant (2001) say little is known about family configurations of individuals with intellectual impairment, and the relational resources that their families provide to them. But the experiences of families with a son or daughter with intellectual disabilities *have* been documented repeatedly in the literature and much of it suggests that for many families there is a continuing struggle to attain the supports that they and their son or daughter require simply to sustain life. This can compromise their capability to nurture relationships (Cottis, 2009). Marie describes how her parents' perception of lurking danger restricted her:

> "I thought they were my friends but I was young then. I was a bit naïve. After that my parents got protective kind of. Like one time I met these people in the park and I thought they were my friends and they said they were going to a disco and I said to mum 'Can I go to the disco?' She said 'No no it's not right you know. Dangerous.' And I tried to go and they said 'No'."

The rejection and isolation experienced by families is documented exhaustively in the parental accounts in Rolph et al (2005). The negativity starts at birth with the way parents are informed about their child's disability. The messages families receive about their children are powerful and negative. Below are just a handful of the legions of stories about this trauma:

> I had my son in 1955. I was just told that he was a mongol and that there would be no future for him, and that he'd probably live no longer than five ... I think I spent the first two years crying. (Nickson, 2005, p 77)

> The doctor looked at Marilyn and he said to me 'You've got a cabbage. Go home and have another child' ... I was crying by this time. (Croucher, 2005, p 143)

> [The doctor] said 'He'll never talk. You'll be banging your head against a brick wall trying to get him to talk.' I said to him 'It's not true. I bet I make him talk' – and he's talking

> now, isn't he. So they were wrong, weren't they? (Mr and Mrs York, 2005, p 165)

The stories families tell are of brutal communication, of shock and sometimes denial, of rejection or unwelcome sympathy from friends and family, and of entering a confusing, often hostile, world of 'special' provision. There is a consistency to these stories that is hard to credit. Is the entire medical profession really so ham-fisted and heartless? Or are the stories an acceptable metaphor for the deep disappointment parents feel when the wished-for child does not materialise. Whatever the source, it means many families live with what one mother termed 'an unhealed wound' (quoted in Rolph and Atkinson, forthcoming).

The impact this disappointment has on people with intellectual disabilities has been described by Valerie Sinason as a secondary handicap:

> At the root, the understandable widespread wish for medical science to eradicate learning disability means that those born and living 'with it' are not emotionally welcomed or included. (Sinason, 2003, p xiii)

Both Sinason (1992) and Niedecken (2003) come at the issue of family relationships through the lens of psychoanalytic psychotherapy. At a primitive unspoken level, they argue, mothers are blamed for producing 'monsters', and disabled children internalise the wish of those around them that they had never been born. This is frequently expressed in behaviour such as self-injury, smearing, rocking, screaming 'that cover the true self from even more hurt' (Sinason, 2003, p xvi), but also make it even more difficult to make contact. The idea that 'success' comes in the form of a job or shiny new home can only add to the sense of failure if it does not lead to greater happiness. As Sinason memorably puts it: 'The new beautiful community homes provide an even more disconcerting backdrop for communications of despair' (Sinason, 2003, p xvi).

If, as we surmise following Sinason and Niedecker, you are feeling rejected or devalued or not equal even when you are loved how does this affect your capacity to form relationships with others? And this is particularly important because for people with intellectual disabilities relationships are the only way to survive in an often hostile world (Edgerton, 1967; Cottis, 2009). So families struggle both with their own sense of difference and rejection, their 'unhealed wound', and that of their disabled sons and daughters (Rolph and Atkinson, forthcoming).

The struggle of families to provide the basics frequently does not give them the resources of time and imagination to foster relationships or to support their family member to have them (Widmer at al, 2008). Marie's parents were only too aware of the risk their daughter ran in going to a disco. Understandably they opted for safety. Marie's need for relationships and a sense of belonging to her peer group was lower on their list of priorities.

Perhaps inevitably, we repeat the plea that families and services work together to build relationships, for themselves, and for their son or daughter, rather than pull in different directions. Working with families implies a different emphasis in staff roles than those currently espoused (Rapley, 2003a; Finlay et al, 2008), a discussion we take up below.

Building social capital?

We referred above to the possibility that social capital might be a valuable way of thinking about building relationships and belonging. Social capital is a multi-dimensional concept that refers both to the quality and structure of social networks (Stone et al, 2003, p 3). The quality of social relationships refers to the extent to which they are characterised by trust and reciprocity. A dense network is one in which social relationships exist between all parties. Such networks are more likely to enforce group norms and homogeneity (Coleman, 1988). Heterogeneous networks are less characterised by trust and reciprocity, but regarded as having the potential to give members access to a wider range of resources.

There are numerous examples in intellectual disability of dense homogeneous networks. The growth of parents' groups in the 1950s and 1960s is one. Rolph traced the history of six Mencap groups in East Anglia, England (2005b). As a consequence of stigma, most families were very isolated with their shame. Rene Harris, whose son was born in 1941 commented: 'You see, you don't think it happens to anyone else' (Harris, 2005, p 48).

The parents' societies were motivated by the perception of exclusion, and the response was to fight for special settings that fostered a sense of belonging, both for the people with intellectual disabilities, and their families. Clubs, nurseries, holidays and outings sponsored and managed by members all featured in the oral accounts collected by Rolph (2005b). Numerous were the testimonials from members to the importance of the relationships and sense of belonging offered by these local societies:

> The Society helped us. We'd lost our son – he'd gone to Little Plumstead Hospital. We had the support of other parents. We made friends – and we threw ourselves into it. It filled a big gap. (Connie Rose, quoted in Rolph, 2005a, p 39)

The societies offered opportunities to share the 'unhealed wound', to resist and to fight back. In social capital terms, the societies represented 'bonding', connections between people with common interests and characteristics, and a sense of purpose, to gain a better life for their children. These networks were often dense, with high levels of trust and reciprocity. There is also evidence that these societies were able to develop bridging relationships, putting pressure on local authorities, for example, to open community-based facilities (Nickson, 2005), or engaging local students as volunteers at social clubs (Rolph, 2005a).

In turning our backs on such groupings as part of a past and discredited era, the argument is that while they were valuable for some families, they excluded others, and were perceived as restrictive for people with intellectual disabilities, condemning them to eternal child status, where much social contact depended on families long after the life stage when most adults had moved on to create their own social networks. There is plentiful evidence in Rolph's work of restrictions that sustained the 'eternal child', for example strict rules about early bedtimes on society holidays. Nevertheless, people with intellectual disabilities as well as family members appeared to have enjoyed the sense of belonging and community associated with, for example, group holidays. These local societies represented an opportunity to have social ties, knowing and being known by others, but in a context in which people were framed by, indeed gained membership because of, their intellectual disability label. The renaissance of some parental networks in the 21st century, such as PLAN in Canada, indicates the enduring need for such bonded forms of social capital.

Such groups are not part of the current vision in which autonomous adults live independent lives in their own homes, employing their own support and enjoying the benefits of paid work and 'inclusion' (Grant and Ramcharan, 2005), with families at arm's length. Not only is this not a picture of what is, rather than what policy makers wish it to be, it is not, we would propose, desirable. We are not quite ready to accept that such bonded networks have no value.

Self-advocacy groups as social capital

Self-advocacy groups are another example of bonded social networks, framed by intellectual disability. Marie commented positively about her group:

> "The self-advocacy group Josephine started meant a lot to me. It was kind of something I could speak up about. All those people with me you know. [It began] I think it was in 1996. We went to People First self-advocacy group in the UK.
>
> "Josephine pushed me I think, and that was good. You know what I mean? Gave me more ideas, stretched me a bit."

Unlike most segregated networks, self-advocacy groups have been praised rather than condemned (Simons, 1992; Buchanan and Walmsley, 2006). On the face of it this is strange. After all, although members frequently decry labels with slogans like 'Label jars not people' (Dowse, 2009, p 571) (see Chapter Four and Palmer et al, 1999), membership is claimed on the grounds of that label, rather like the parents' groups discussed earlier. They differ from most forms of segregation, such as hospitals, day centres and special schools, in the sense that membership is voluntary rather than forced or by default, and that they are, at least in name, controlled by the membership (Tilley, 2006). Certainly, individuals appear to enjoy self-advocacy groups, frequently as much for their social possibilities as for their political campaigning. Tilley observed of members' perspectives on Talkback, the advocacy organisation she researched, that Talkback was valued because it was fun and a source of social networks (2006, p 258), just as people involved in parents' groups recollected the fun associated with group holidays and social clubs (Rolph, 2005b). This point was also made by Chapman (2005).

Viewed in social capital terms, self-advocacy groups, and other such associations of people with intellectual disabilities, are a form of bonding on the basis of a set of ascribed characteristics and commonality of experience that give people common ground. Riddell et al (1999, p 64) argue that there must be protected space for social capital to be developed by people with intellectual disabilities, and that from this understanding people will then be able to engage in bridging relationships and rejoin mainstream social life. Certainly these bonded groups appear to give people the strength to develop an alternative narrative to that of failure and rejection. They can provide a space in which the painful experiences of being unwanted, segregated and bullied can be shared. In this extract from a life story, 'Alice in Wonderland: My Life', 'Alice' is a graphic example:

> They call me mad. My family SHOWING off theirselves, they're better than me. Blame me for everything that goes on in a day's time. My mum puts things in a place, she doesn't remember what she does in a day's time, so everything is missing, all the blame is *Alice took it* ...
>
> Throw my mum in the dustbin if you like ... I'm a sick person, I can't do nothing, I'm a crippled person. Just call me back a cripple, a dirty crippled tramp that doesn't even wash herself ... I only do it when she gone away ... I'm forever out, going places to be out of her sight. To get rid of her screaming and shouting. (Alice, 1999, p 120)

Alice fought off her family's negativity, as her story shows. It took courage, energy, and, above all, the support provided by her peer group to do this.

Such bonded groups *can* provide a relatively secure basis from which to build bridging relationships, both with individuals and with other non-disabled organisations. But this is not always the case. The capability to do this requires relatively sophisticated stewardship. One established self-advocacy group with which one of the authors has long been associated has rejected any role for non-disabled people other than their paid support workers. This appears to limit their options to build relationships with others that could in turn build social capital.

Others with a less rigid view of what constitutes 'user control' furnish examples of what can be achieved through alliances. The Changing Our Lives Hidden History Research Group, a group of young people with intellectual disabilities, researched the history of long-stay hospitals during 2009. They commented:

> We never knew about this history of people with learning disabilities. We realised that if we had been born 20 years ago some of us would have been living in long stay hospitals. (Changing Our Lives, forthcoming)

The project took them out to meet and interview both staff and residents of former long-stay hospitals, to build relationships with others interested in this history, both with intellectual disabilities, such as Mabel Cooper, but also academics and media experts, and to present at conferences and workshops. The work they did fostered a sense of belonging and identity, not only at the level of the (supported) team they formed, with bonds of solidarity and friendship, but also with a wider community of people with intellectual disabilities, past and present. As they commented in their account of the Hidden History project: 'We don't always think segregation is bad. It can help people feel safe. But too much of it isn't good, and people should have a choice' (Changing our Lives, forthcoming).

Just as other groups in society, such as women and same-sex attracted people, have formed separately to both bond together and to take political action, so this too should be part of the work of creating belonging.

Workforce implications

If, as we have argued in this chapter, building and sustaining relationships, both bonding and bridging relationships, which support belonging and build on people's histories, is at the heart of a good life, what does this mean for those whose work, paid or unpaid, is to support people with intellectual disabilities? Richardson and Richie (1989) identify two approaches that can promote the formation of friendships as 'increasing opportunities to meet others' (p 40): befriending schemes, citizen advocacy schemes and social clubs; and 'increasing the ability to make friends' (p 51): skills training, confidence-building, emotional literacy and giving help to others.

The workforce we have is ill-prepared to undertake such tasks. Rapley (2003b) identified three categories of staff–resident interaction in order of frequency: babying/parenting; instruction-giving; and collaborating/pedagogy. Finlay et al (2008, p 350) observed:

> Our research to date illustrates how power is a dominant feature of interactions between people with learning disabilities and those employed to support them, to such an extent that even in forums set up to provide opportunities for service users to speak out subtle interactional dynamics may act to disempower them.

Roy McConkey commented:

> Services remain as they always have been because we mistakenly try to isolate, care for or 'fix' the individual with a disability rather than nurture his or her relationships with other people. (2005, p 487)

If the promises of even an ordinary life are to be delivered, then a properly trained and supported workforce with a focus on promoting a good life will be essential. New models of employment are emerging, where staff are employed directly by people with intellectual disabilities, such as direct payments/individualised budgets/user-controlled budgets, and these are considered in Chapter Nine.

Here we focus on the current workforce and argue that as it is constituted it is unlikely to deliver on policy goals of inclusion, or have the capability to promote the core elements of a good life we have identified. Data on the social care workforce in England (people who work with older people and people with intellectual disabilities) (Skills for Care, 2007) showed that conditions of work are poor. Pay was low at £6.87 per hour, furthermore:

- 62% lack pensions;
- 25% reported unpaid overtime (p 28);
- 21% did not have time to do everything expected of them (p 31);
- 45% did not have travel costs met (p 35); and
- 23% reported that they were not supervised at all (p 36), rising to 38% of those who work in client's homes.

Given that this was a generic survey of the entire social care workforce, not specific to intellectual disability, conclusions need to be tentative. However, it is striking that the tasks staff report undertaking in this survey are overwhelmingly what we might term 'tending' rather than supporting choice, independence and inclusion as envisaged in *Valuing people* and its successor *Valuing people now*, let alone nurturing relationships (see Figure 1).

Of all the 10 top-mentioned tasks, only the last might conceivably cover anything other than the first of Nussbaum's capabilities. The predominance of tending tasks over and above interacting with residents was noted by Finlay et al (2008, p 351):

> In this service cleanliness and routine seemed to be the primary concerns of the staff, even taking precedence over engaging with the residents in either a social or task based manner.... In this home most staff members would also not routinely encourage residents to participate in the preparation of their meals, in part because of fears over food 'hygiene' and in part because they saw the residents as lacking the skills required.

Figure 1: Activities on the job

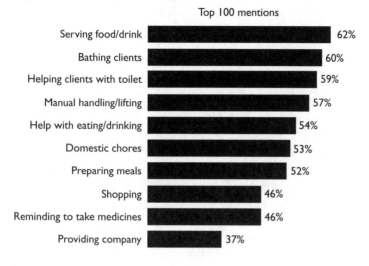

Top 100 mentions

Activity	Percentage
Serving food/drink	62%
Bathing clients	60%
Helping clients with toilet	59%
Manual handling/lifting	57%
Help with eating/drinking	54%
Domestic chores	53%
Preparing meals	52%
Shopping	46%
Reminding to take medicines	46%
Providing company	37%

Base: All jobs done by care workers (514)
Source: Q17

Change in the light of prevailing employment patterns in social care will be hard. A survey on the implications of outsourcing services to the private and not-for-profit sectors indicated that there were 30,000 employers for around 1 million staff working in social care in England (Social Care Workforce Unit, 2008). The authors of this study comment that 'the sector faces a workforce employed on a much more casual basis' (p 8) with associated challenges of recruiting and retaining good staff. Casually employed staff, staff who change rapidly, are a poor basis for supporting a good life, however defined, for themselves or the people they work with.

If staff and unpaid supporters are to help people towards a good life, we will need people skilled in community development, who will search out opportunities for bridging relationships; people who will work with families, rather than despite or against them, to support their capabilities to nurture relationships; and people who are prepared to enter into 'accepting relationships' (Taylor and Bogdan, 1989; Clapton, 2009), willing to hear people's stories, however told, and offer a sense of relationship and promote and value belonging. It is a long way from where we are now, but clarity over what people are expected to deliver, and how, if a good life is to be promoted, is a start.

NINE

Promoting a good life

Introduction

> Fortunately the feebleminded are much more easily made happy than a sane person. (Mary Dendy, quoted in McDonagh, 2008, p 321)

> "I think staff need training to be more confident, you know, and to speak the right way to me, you know, 'cos some of them can be a bit bossy you know. I think they need to really put their feet in my shoes, kind of." (Marie Wolfe)

In this chapter we continue our consideration of the implications of working towards a good life for the roles of those who support people with intellectual disabilities. Here we focus on the idea of independence, one that is prominent in current thinking (see DH, 2009).

We continue to stress the centrality of relationships, and consider what kinds of relationships are needed to promote a good life for people with intellectual disabilities. In doing this we put forward an argument that in current thinking staff are cast as a way to compensate for people's perceived lack of reason. This has consequences for staff roles, for training and the underpinning values and philosophy to inform practice, which simply are not in place.

To recap, in Chapter Three we observed:

> Given the strong focus on the importance of reason in philosophical thought about a good life, what are the consequences for groups of people whose reason is perceived as flawed, impaired or 'inferior' to those around them? Does this preclude them from leading a 'good life'? (p 49)

If we accept the centrality of reason to a 'good life' then we really do have a problem. Rather than face this conundrum, we believe that ingenious efforts have been made to make up for the perceived lack of reason by constructing relationships that will compensate. They are part of what Dowse described as:

> Technologies of agency or citizenship seek to enhance and improve the individual's capacities for participation and action and thereby assist them in becoming actors capable of managing risk. (Dowse, 2009, p 577)

If these fail, then we can blame others rather than consider the problem posed by the perceived impaired reason. For example, in the quotation below 'dependency' is 'created' by failure to personalise support:

> support is often not fitted to the individual, rather disabled people are expected to fit into existing services; services tend to focus on incapacity, inability and risk, with the result that dependency is created. (Prime Minister's Strategy Unit, 2005, *Improving the life chances of disabled people*, quoted in Finlay et al, 2008, p 349)

Similarly, in discussing research relationships, Dan Goodley asked whether ability is 'a reflection of support networks, rather than some individual quality or deficiency' (2000, p 52). In other words, he would say, it is a researcher's responsibility to make research accessible and meaningful for people with intellectual disabilities. It is the researcher's job to make things right.

The belief that if we can get relationships and support right, the impact of intellectual impairment will disappear and enable the achievement of a good life, is a logical extension of thinking within both the social model of disability with its stress on reducing barriers to inclusion, and in social role valorisation by the postulation that enhancing someone's competence and image can reduce or eliminate stigma. The result has been that unrealistic expectations have been placed on solutions, such as individual budgets, which see structural change as the 'tool' for change management, with new roles, such as personal assistants, whose task is to make up for the space left by the impairment.

Yet relationships *are* critical in all sorts of ways, even if they do not promote independence or compensate for perceived impairments. Commitment to others, and the wisdom that comes from a life lived with and for others, were described in Chapter Two as central, as was the issue of friendship. Freud placed love and work as the key foundations of a good life, and we defined these concepts broadly in terms of relationships and meaning in life, rather than in terms of sexual relationships or 'paid work'. As discussed in the previous chapter, leading a meaningful life and one linked with others through relationships has been difficult to achieve (Atkinson and Ward, 1987; McConkey, 2005). In spite of the extensive policy and practice changes, the current emphases on inclusion and, at least in the UK, on personalisation (DH, 2007a), there still seems to be a gap between what is hoped for in policies and what people have (Emerson et al, 2005; Grant and Ramcharan, 2005). This gap is often due to a failure to consider what kinds of relationships people with intellectual disabilities may want or need in order to lead good lives, and how they might be developed (Arthur, 2003; McConkey, 2005). As McConkey (2005, p 469) commented: 'Of all the assessments done on people with learning disabilities the one least likely to be carried out is an examination of their friendships'.

The emphasis in policy on 'independence' in particular seems to have been unhelpful, borrowed from thinking in disability studies and assumptions inherent in Western philosophy about what it means to be fully human, without proper consideration of what it might mean for people with intellectual disabilities.

Not only is it difficult to envisage a future in which people achieve jobs, independence and meaningful citizenship, if indeed these remain the underpinnings of a good life, without substantial ongoing support to bridge the gap between where people are and where they want to be (Townson et al, 2004), research and evidence from many people with intellectual disabilities indicate that relationships are more than a means to achieve independence. Such relationships do include the need for support: 'Having support when and if we need it to organise activities, and to participate in them. This support might be from support staff, family and friends' (Aird et al, 2009, p 72).

But they go beyond the 'mechanics of support'. Relationships are essential to a sense of 'social inclusion' and belonging (Tideman, 2005; Kearney with Johnson, 2009), to being accepted and having opportunities simply to talk to or communicate with people (McConkey and Collins, 2009). They also include the ways in which we are related to by significant others in our lives, such as family. Here we are arguing for a recovery of a strand of thinking in intellectual disability that has consistently argued the importance of friendship, ties and connections since the closure of institutions began in the 1980s (see, for example, Atkinson and Ward, 1987; Firth and Rapley, 1990; Smyth and McConkey, 2003; McConkey and Collins, 2009).

The importance of this needs to be reiterated in the present context of regarding workers as silent technological aids (Meyer et al, 2007).

For people with intellectual disabilities, and those who seek to support them in becoming self-realising to the maximum of their potential, getting relationships sorted seems critical to success. But they will never entirely compensate for or obliterate the impairment. Rather than seek relationships that counteract the impairment, we need to find ways to support people on a journey that leads them to be able to say truthfully that their life is good. We propose that a little more honesty about the real challenges might just be helpful.

A failed relationship

We begin with a story that, we believe, highlights some fundamental challenges in relationships. This is what happened when I decided to offer my services as an advocate.

Jan writes:

> One of the most difficult things I have ever tried to do was to be an advocate. My advocacy partner whom I shall call Richard was a young black man of 18 who was living in a residential school, and who was due to leave in the next few months. His distant local authority had taken no steps to plan his future, and my task was to help him make choices within the constraints of what they would pay for and, although I had not appreciated this when I agreed to be his advocate, within the constraints of how his parents saw his future. Richard seemed to be a troubled young man. He had no speech, and used no sign language I could recognise. He was on medication for epilepsy, and for depression. He poked his eyes a lot.
>
> Meeting him to get to know him even a little was difficult. He had no phone, so I relied on care staff to let me know whether the times I proposed to visit were convenient to him and to them. They often forgot to respond. When I did get to see him we were obliged to meet in the living area of the six-bedded house where he lived, unless a member of staff was available to accompany us to the grounds or to the pub. It was not within his risk assessment for me to go anywhere alone with him. His fellow residents were equally troubled, and finding a quiet space was immensely difficult.

I did never feel I knew Richard, let alone helped him work out what he might want out of his adult life. The whole process was one of compromise. I found a placement I thought suitable, not too far from where his family lived. It was a home in a suburb, with a lived in sort of garden with nearby shops, cafes and pubs, and where residents appeared to have personalised their own rooms. Richard never saw it because there was never a staff member free to accompany us to visit the place, an hour distant. His parents did not agree with this proposal. There was a hole in the garden fence, and they were concerned that this was not a safe place for their son. In the end a placement was agreed in a new and very expensive privately run property with fitted carpets and en suite bathrooms. It had a block of flats on one side, a large supermarket and car park on the other, a busy dual carriageway in front and a high fence surrounding it. By no stretch of the imagination was there any likelihood of Richard finding a 'local community' in the immediate vicinity. To me it would have felt like living death to be there – but it was not my life and I lacked any grounds for insisting on my preferred choice. At that point I abandoned my role. Five years on I've not built the courage to try again.

In approaching my work with Richard I had abandoned many of the skills I possess and use in my daily life. With a non-disabled 18 year old, in a disadvantaged position, I would have tried to become a mentor, build confidence, share information, open her eyes to possibilities. I brought a different mindset to Richard, one which said I must subjugate my own judgement and seek to substitute his as if he were capable of rational and informed decision making. Even if this was the proper underpinning of my task, there were many barriers:

- The difficulty of communication with someone who uses no sophisticated form of 'language'.
- The challenge of getting to know someone within the constraints of rigid service systems, including 'risk management'.
- The limits of what is available, affordable and what Richard can imagine for himself.
- The complex web of stakeholders involved in the lives of people like Richard, most of whom have a view on what a 'good life' should look like for another person.
- The all too frequent marginalisation of families by well-intentioned others.

What this rather painful experience of failure taught me was that being an advocate is not straightforward. I would rate it as one of the most difficult tasks I have ever taken on. And yet, it is written about, indeed I have personally written about it, as if it were simply a matter of being independent, being a skilled communicator, being willing to put aside one's own judgement in favour of the partner's, having the right sort of intentions (Simons, 1993).

We go on to discuss how Richard's story illuminates the challenges workers face in developing relationships that are premised on their role as making up for the impairment. We then reflect on the composition and training of the workforce currently. Finally, we return to Richard's story and paint an alternative picture that might just have worked better.

Support workers and advocates

Following the principle of 'independence', the tenets of citizen advocacy that I brought to my work with Richard – being on the side of the person, suspending my own views while seeking to promote his, seeking to compensate for the impact of his impairments – have been translated extensively into modernised support worker roles.

Yet advocacy roles have been little studied (Gray and Jackson, 2002). Liz Tilley, who researched two advocacy organisations in southern England for her PhD thesis, explored possible reasons for this silence:

> Citizen advocacy, which was probably the first model of advocacy to become established in the UK, has an inherent suspicion of academic research. It is felt that to research advocacy is to treat it as an 'intervention' and to 'clientise' those it supports, thereby thwarting a key aim of citizen advocacy, which is to promote partners' access to and acceptance within, the life of the community. Second, the stress laid upon confidentiality by all models of advocacy has led to an understandable reluctance to discuss actual advocacy processes in the public arena. (Tilley, 2006, p 15)

Thus, information about the intricate workings of advocacy relationships that might have helped to prepare me more effectively for the role has been occluded. This occlusion has not been helpful as advocacy has informed a number of new roles in intellectual disability.

Staff failings are frequently blamed for the failure to achieve ambitious policy goals, as noted earlier. These views are echoed in numerous research reports where poor staff training and practices are held responsible for restricted and impoverished lives (see, for example, Robertson et al, 2001; McConkey et al, 2005; Commission for Healthcare Audit and Inspection, 2007; Finlay et al, 2008). There is undoubtedly truth in these assertions, but, we would argue, it is a partial truth. Excuses can be made on grounds of resources. As noted in Chapter Eight, pay and conditions are poor, support is largely confined to 'tending' to people's basic needs for food, shelter and physical health, and abuse continues to be detected. But, we contend, this is only part of the story. A lack of clarity about what might constitute a 'good life', about what is expected, what might be achieved and how, also contribute to these repeated failings. The literature on successful organisations indicates that it is critically important that staff know what is expected of them, that these expectations can be readily communicated and that they are achievable (Clement and Bigby, 2009). There is often a vision expressed in government policies, for example *Valuing people now* (DH, 2009) in the UK. But the gap between the vision and the tools at people's disposal to help realise that vision is wide. And we are less than certain that the vision of relationships as having the function of making up for the perceived absence of reason, just as a wheelchair makes up for a mobility impairment, is either desirable or attainable.

Self-advocacy support

A new role that has attracted remarkably little attention, despite its centrality in the self-advocacy movement, is that of support worker in self-advocacy organisations. Self-advocacy, as discussed in Chapter Four, has had a central place in progressive thinking about learning disability, variously described as 'finding a voice' or a 'new social movement'. Non-disabled support workers play a crucial part in these organisations. The ideal is that self-advocacy supporters are directly employed by their organisation's members, an ideal articulated as early as 1989 in Bronach Crawley's UK survey of self-advocacy groups.

Chapman attributes this to the influence of the social model of disability, which argued for self-determination, and models of providing support that were under the control of disabled people (see, for example, Morris, 1993). No longer was it acceptable to be an ally, the self-advocacy membership needed to be in control, to be independent. Simone Aspis, a woman labelling herself as a 'disabled woman with intellectual disabilities' (Aspis, 2000), questioned the motivations of non-disabled people. She wrote: 'We attract support-workers who do not understand any form of oppression ... oh God!' (Aspis, 2001).

There has been if anything more of a silence around the role of self-advocacy support workers than there has been around the practice of advocacy, perhaps reflecting that these people are expected to be technologies of agency like wheelchairs, Braille or replacement hands. You do not need to train a wheelchair, or expect it to have views and opinions. Furthermore, in an ideal world they would not be needed.

The silence about the role, indeed the silence expected of people carrying out the role, has led to camouflaging tactics that obscure its inherent contradictions. Rohhss Chapman, herself a former self-advocacy support worker, conducted an extensive piece of research for her PhD into the role of support workers in self-advocacy (2001–05). She worked throughout with the Carlisle Research Cooperative, a group of people with intellectual disabilities, itself an example of the new types of relationship between non-disabled and disabled people, to be discussed below. She writes:

> The research showed that the self-advocacy support role was an inherently ambiguous and contradictory role. Although there was apparent energy, enthusiasm and commitment it was shown that this needed to be harnessed and channelled into effective means of providing support, if a group was to adhere to their own rhetoric around 'People First philosophy'. Many of the workers appeared to be busy 'doing their own thing'. This was largely without reference to the ideas and requests of their employers. (Chapman, 2005, p 72)

This finding was echoed by Tilley in her research into two advocacy organisations, who found that the rhetoric of users being in the driving seat was subscribed to in theory, but did not match the reality:

> There were certainly occasions in which non-disabled members of staff appeared to be narrating themselves out of their roles. This may be a result of organisational values which emphasised equality and user control. The very notion of 'leaders' – particularly if they do not have intellectual disabilities – may be seen by some members to eschew such principles. The staff team at Talkback stressed the role played by *all* members in the running of Talkback, and in this way can be seen to adhere to Block's (1993)

notion of a collection of 'stewards' guiding and shaping the group's future. However, the accounts by people with intellectual disabilities and the Talkback chair suggested that staff members – and more specifically the chief executive – were perceived as being leading figures within the organisation. (Tilley, 2006, p 402)

The job of support in a user-controlled organisation is undoubtedly complex. Chapman writes of two inherent contradictions, the first being the tension between supporting the organisation to function effectively and meeting the needs individuals have for support. In this regard, support workers frequently had a well-nigh impossible job, being expected to help people to the toilet at one level, to teach people the intricacies of budgeting and contracting at another, at the same time as supporting their self-advocate employers to manage the organisation's wider relationships.

The second tension was role confusion. Support workers are there to support people to be empowered or independent, and yet these very same people are their employers. The workers in Chapmans research lacked the sorts of support that might help them achieve the difficult balance:

> support-workers supported the very people who managed and employed them, thus creating a largely unique and uncharted position for both parties.... This, then, was no ordinary job, but one of multiple roles, where boundaries were blurred.... It was, however, hard for them [support workers] to do this without effective supervisory and training structures, which, in the main, the groups simply did not have. (Chapman, 2005, p 367)

Members varied in their expectations, but leading self-advocates argued that the workers were there to meet the members' needs, facilitating rather than leading. If members did not understand what was going on, the support worker was responsible. The role was:

> Bridg[ing] the gap between the (largely inaccessible) outside world and what members wanted to do for themselves ... this also implied that issues of impairment could be counteracted by the support-worker, enabling the members to proceed without stumbling over the constant barriers that were around them in everyday life.

> Members wanted protection, but also no interference; management, but also ownership. Members spoke about how they were in control of the groups, but did not seem to be aware that a lot of the decisions over how the organisation ran were out of their hands. Members did not want support–workers to 'take over' but nor did they want the 'total power shutdown' described by Dowson (1990). (Chapman, 2005, p 112)

These tensions in the relationship expectations set up by the principles of user control borrowed from physical disability have often been glossed over in the literature. As Tilley commented in concluding her research into two advocacy groups:

> In particular, the literature was ambiguous on the subject of who actually runs advocacy groups – arguably an uncomfortable question for organisations driven by agendas of service user autonomy and control. (Tilley, 2006, p 401)

People working in self-advocacy support carry a burden of impossible expectations, frequently in under-resourced organisations. My picture of them is of silent and underpaid people striving to achieve the impossible, to be the bridge across which the members walk as they realise themselves, build skills in budgeting and develop political astuteness, while simultaneously ensuring that the demands of the 'real world' – for health and safety, budgets and so on – are met.

Personal assistant roles

There is increasing support for the idea, similar to the arguments for user-controlled advocacy groups, that user control in the employment of personal assistants fosters a good life by increasing autonomy (Duffy, 2006; Leece and Bornat, 2006). With origins both in advocacy and in the Independent Living Movement, personal assistant roles are characterised by an aspiration to transfer power from workers to disabled people by making disabled people the employers, rather than the clients.

The move to individual budgets, where the person who uses services is the employer, has been seen as a way to put the user in control (Morris, 2004; Duffy, 2006). It has been described as encapsulating 'new social relations of support' (Prideaux et al, 2009, p 557) and there is evidence that what are sometimes called 'cash for care' models deliver considerable social benefits for people who use services (Stainton and

Boyce, 2004; Hatton, 2008), as well as for family members/informal carers who report positively on the value of increased flexibility and who, in a number of schemes, can themselves be paid for their services (Blyth and Gardner, 2007).

This is another model pioneered by people with physical disabilities (Morris, 1993; Campbell, 2006; Glasby et al, 2006) and transferred to people with learning difficulties. Such schemes have received fairly universal acclaim (Stainton and Boyce, 2004; Blyth and Gardner, 2007; Hatton, 2008; Prideaux et al, 2009). The relatively limited empirical research undertaken into relationships between user/employers and personal assistants indicates, however, that changing the economic power does not in itself obviate the need for negotiation over roles and relationships between the assistant or worker and the user. It is not simply a case of finding a technology, in the form of a person, which makes up for the space created by the impairment. Empirical studies of schemes where physically disabled people employ personal assistants shed some light on emerging issues.

A Canadian research study conducted with people who rely on mechanical ventilation (PVUs) and their paid personal support workers indicated that there is a balance to be struck between the task and the relational aspects of care, caring for and caring about (Gibson et al, 2009). Some PVUs indeed regarded their support workers as the equivalent of technical support, purely instrumental mechanisms to carry out practical tasks: 'We use the attendants as our own hands. They do things we can't do. And basically you give them directions' (Gibson et al, 2009, p 322).

Another used a strikingly non-human metaphor, describing them as 'being similar to a steel frame inside a modern building. It does support the frame but is not visible to the naked eye' (p 323). Others were more aware of the importance of relationship: 'They're people, you can't forget they're people. They have knowledge too. They're not old shoes' (p 324). Significantly, this PVU talked of 'asking' rather than 'directing' his assistants.

Workers in this same study made observations about relationships with their employers. Lorne commented: 'Some clients, not all, refer to us as "their staff". And that irritates me. Cause I don't think of them as "staff"' (p 325). Cheryl, a worker, commented: 'Oh, sometimes they see us as machines, I think, sometimes they think about themselves, they don't think about you. You have to remind them, I'm only human, I need a break' (p 322).

There are indications in this study that in the name of promoting independence there is a distinct likelihood of 'user oppression' being replaced by the oppression and depersonalisation of workers. The authors conclude:

> The consumer-directed approach is a necessary but insufficient foundation for assistance relationships ... the best of which were characterized by mutual respect, and acknowledgment that each side depends on the other. (p 327)

An Australian study also drew on the analogy of the assistant 'taking the place of my hands' in the view of user/employers with physical disabilities, who actively disliked assistants with technical expertise, preferring to train them in what worked best for them (Meyer et al, 2007). These studies focused on relatively able and articulate users, where being someone's hands was the dominant metaphor. Replacement hands is a metaphor that, like the steel frame, portrays the assistant as akin to a mechanical aid (Meyer et al, 2007). However, to carry this analogy further into the intellectual disabilities realm would place the assistant as a replacement or adjunct for the brain, a startling phenomenon, more familiar in science fiction than in social theory.

Working as a personal assistant for a person with intellectual disabilities can be rather a different proposition. David Schelley's reflective account of his experience of working as a personal assistant to 'SW' is a rare personal reflexive account, which also highlights the complex challenges faced by people trying to work as technologies that fill the gap created by the impairment. Schelley proposes that reflexivity should ask the question 'What is?' rather than 'What ought to be?' (Schelley, 2008, p 720).

SW is described as 'a 22 year old individual with intellectual disability and mild autism' (p 720). Schelley's account of his attempts to 'include' SW and promote his independence and capacity to make choices is troubling, and he comes to troubling conclusions. He describes himself as beginning by believing 'I can provide a better life for SW' (p 721) due to his knowledge of disability and autism, his reading of Wolfensberger's principles of integration and personalisation, and his positive intentions. Who amongst us has not been guilty, as I was in relation to Richard, of believing we can do better, empower and understand more than predecessors, colleagues or parents. As the year progressed, Schelley came to the conclusion that SW was different, thought differently and understood differently than him. Despite his original intentions to promote SW's independence, he acknowledges that a father–son-type relationship with SW emerged, and argues that this improved

SW's quality of life more than his early efforts to enable choice. 'Either the literature was wrong, I thought, or I was a bad personal assistant' (p 729). He struggles with his finding as a practitioner that choice, empowerment and self-determination were not only unachievable for SW, they did not improve the quality of his life. He asks whether:

> The postulation that individuals with intellectual disability think differently than individuals without intellectual disability aggravates a fear that we will assume people with intellectual disabilities have inherent deficiencies and that we will return to institutionalisation. (p 729)

Schelley's conclusion is that the much-despised medical model can help by allowing for an appreciation of difference. Denial of difference does no favours, either to the people on the receiving end of ill-conceived policies, or to staff who are cast into a role that guarantees eternal failure when performance is compared to the glossy ideals reflected in policy and in organisational names like 'Alternative Futures'.

Is this a counsel of despair? It certainly indicates that the apparently simple act of allocating control to people through casting them as employers, and giving them the material wherewithal to take on that role, is not in itself an answer to the problem of support that fails to foster a 'good life'. However, if we allow that support is about enabling someone to move from where they are to where they want to be, then difference can be allowed for, and guidance offered with respect for the learner as an adult, can be allowed.

The Norah Fry Research Centre undertook a qualitative study of 19 people who had personal assistants. The people with intellectual disabilities were very positive about the benefits:

> to feel 'in control' of their own support. Independent living often means to them that they can do more things without support, but it also means that they can choose exactly when to do something. (Williams with West of England Centre for Inclusive Living, 2007, p 16)

People who had formerly lived in residential care were able to identify very stark differences:

> felt that they had achieved their dream of being 'free' and in charge of their own life. The particular things they liked about their 1:1 support were to do with good relationships

and trust. (Williams with West of England Centre for Inclusive Living, 2007, p 16)

The rather simplistic 'hands' analogy does not translate for people with intellectual disabilities. Personal assistants were valued because they could double as friends, to be with on social occasions, to extend social networks, to introduce new activities: 'They in fact appreciated a good deal of "friendliness" with their PA, and many used PA support to increase their own social opportunities' (Williams with West of England Centre for Inclusive Living, 2007).

Striking a balance between allowing people to make choices, and guidance, was one of the most challenging aspects to get right:

> In addition, people did like their supporters to be proactive on their behalf, and to 'extend their lives', without doing too much and taking over. They were aware that all this demanded subtle skills on the part of their PA and support workers, and that the best way was for them to talk things over together. Many PAs and people with learning difficulties emphasised the importance of team work. (Williams with West of England Centre for Inclusive Living, 2007, p 16)

The absence of supervision and training for personal assistants was cited as a significant gap by the research team, as it was for self-advocacy support.

What is striking in the report is the significance of existing family and family networks. People who chose their own assistants were likely to employ someone they already knew, and two employed family members directly. As with Professor Hatton's evaluation of In Control (2008), the best results were achieved with close family involvement.

The *Skills for support* report concluded that the model of educator–learner was of value for these relationships, but that care needs to be taken to ensure that this is based on adult education philosophy, rather than the more traditional and ubiquitous parent–child model (Rapley, 2003a).

Working together: an impossible dream?

There have been dissenting voices, much criticised, who argue that in learning disability, 'user-led' is unrealistic and unprofitable. Craig Dearden argues for a 'partnership':

> We believe that a partnership between people with and without intellectual disabilities is far more effective than a situation in which people with intellectual disabilities are left to do everything on their own.... In my experience, those types of organisations often struggle to deliver, and hit problems in the medium and long term ... I think that is an incredibly slow approach in a competitive charity environment. (Craig Dearden, quoted in Mack, 2001)

Dearden does not explain the nature of the partnership here. But that weasel word seems to be at the centre of it. What might such partnerships look like?

The Carlisle Research Collaborative moved from being a self-advocacy group, in which only the members with intellectual disabilities had a voice, to being a Research Cooperative, where everyone has a voice – including researchers and support workers (Townson et al, 2004). They write: 'A cooperative is a group of people working together to do something they all want to do' (p 75). The work they describe has been about the history of People First. It is a long-established group, and has evolved relationships of trust where it is alright to acknowledge that others have skills the group needs to learn.

In a complementary article, Chapman and McNulty, the non-disabled members of the Cooperative, describe their own roles, arguing 'unless the process of support is clearly out in the open it cannot be challenged by others, or improved upon' (Chapman and McNulty, 2004, p 78). The critical elements were time, to get to know and trust one another, and to allow the people with intellectual disabilities to decide what elements of research they needed or wanted to know about. At the same time, the group told their own stories, and began to develop theories, such that research is 'rejecting' if people are not included from the outset. Rohhss Chapman observed how she moved from being the main driver to becoming an observer as the group evolved its own style.

The story of the Cooperative's journey to becoming a recognised group of specialist researchers is one from which the following lessons can be drawn about the nature of partnerships that can support people to get from where they are to where they want to be:

- Time and trust.
- Sharing expertise – a two-way process.
- Making the process explicit, and checking back regularly that the aims of the group (in this case 'people-led research') are being furthered.

• Reciprocity – disabled people give as well as receive.

Nothing revolutionary here, perhaps, but this 'Cooperative' model challenges the crude model of a user-controlled organisation that rules current thinking. It recognises implicitly that people do have intellectual disabilities, and that the challenge is to find ways of relating that foster a joint endeavour, not premised on the binary of disabled–non-disabled, but on coming together around a common task. We turn now to consider what this discussion may mean for the workforce.

The workforce

If we accept the argument that we need a workforce that will enable people to learn, to move from where they are to where they want to be using an adult educator model, then a properly trained and supervised workforce will be of prime importance.

However, the rhetoric around personal assistants underplays the importance of a trained and supervised workforce (Shakespeare, 2006, Glasby et al, 2006). Some PA employers actively dislike people with qualifications and experience in care-giving (Meyer et al, 2007). The social model implicitly and sometimes explicitly dismisses professionals as self-serving and self-interested (Davis, 2004). In SRV thinking staff should be motivated by attitudes, values and commitment rather than pay, status and career prospects (Walmsley, 2006). And yet, we are asking a lot of staff if the ideals are to be achieved.

Although expectations of staff have changed dramatically, the practice of setting out precisely what staff need to do, and how they should be prepared, supervised and rewarded has not kept pace. As Finlay et al found in an empirical study of working practices in residential homes:

> The abstract level of official discourse is not always, or easily, translated into the concrete level of questioning, encouraging, commanding, chiding or coercing (among other ways that staff engage with residents).
>
> Empowerment does not flow in any straightforward way from changes in service values, structures, planning or inspection regimes. (Finlay et al, 2008, p 350)

Richard Titmuss was indeed prophetic when in 1961 he stated:

> At present, we are drifting into a situation in which, by shifting the emphasis from the institution to the community

– a trend which in principle and with qualifications we all applaud – we are transferring the care of the mentally ill from trained staff to untrained or ill-equipped staff or no staff at all. (Titmuss, 1961, p 356)

Titmuss overstated the case with regard to the presence of qualified staff in then contemporary services. But his assertion has been borne out over time as 'learning difficulties' services migrated into social care, and then further migrated into self-directed support. As these migrations have taken place, so increasingly people are supported by staff with few qualifications, and with no obvious career trajectory. A good life for staff remains elusive.

There has never been a dedicated workforce to support people post-deinstitutionalisation, to support the ethic of inclusion. Mitchell and Welshman state:

> Yet attention to the workforce has been extremely low profile in policy initiatives. Despite community care being a reality for several decades for a large number of people, there has not been a substantial investment in developing a workforce which is fit for the new roles community living requires. (2006, p 187)

The 1971 White Paper 'Better Services' pointed out that the 'need in the hospital services is reorientation of staff originally trained in an older tradition, and the interchange of new ideas and experiences' (DHSS, 1971, para 231).

The 1979 Jay Report developed this argument:

> The staff who care for mentally handicapped persons should be compassionate and caring, but also professionally trained; their role should be to help each mentally handicapped person to develop mentally, physically and emotionally. (Jay, 1979, para 376)

Given these findings, the potential for staff to support the realisation of a good life, either for themselves or the people they work with and for, seems limited.

What would it mean for the workforce?

Jan says:

> I identified my challenges in relating to Richard as an advocate in introducing this chapter. I'd like to conclude by setting out what I now think was needed to make this a relationship that did contribute to a better life for Richard. In approaching the role, I set aside the extensive experience I have of setting up processes that will enable complex and challenging relationships to flourish. I was seduced by the advocacy rhetoric into believing that this was somehow different, a matter of putting myself at his disposal, his person against or in spite of the other people in his life, particularly his family. I treated Richard, and his family, with less skill and empathy than I possess because I was fixated on his disability. I realise now that in order to achieve that desirable goal it was necessary to recognise the range of stakeholders in Richard's future, and to find out their positions: Richard himself, his parents, the teachers in his school, the care staff who were with him every day. I would have needed to get to know them, both to ensure that I was able to add something to what they offered; and as a route to getting to know Richard better. And they needed to know, and trust me.

> Key ingredients:
> - Time and trust.
> - Sharing expertise – a two-way process.
> - Making the process explicit, and checking back regularly that the aims (in this case a good life for Richard) are being furthered.

Conclusion

What, then, can we conclude about the challenge of setting up relationships that need to be in place to support people achieving a good, or even slightly better, life? We return to the idea so nicely coined by the Carlisle Research cooperative, that 'Support is a role that bridges the gap between what people want to be doing, and what they are rejected from doing by the way things are' (Townson et al, 2004, p 84).

Is this a helpful vision? Only, we contend, if we acknowledge difference, and are prepared to allow people to define their own version of a good life, rather than that imposed by rhetoric, which insists that if we can get the environment right, a good life will follow; and only if we abandon the unhelpful fiction that people working in support roles are merely technological aids to make good the space left by the impairment. We like the vision that the energies and goodwill of all involved in people's lives can be harnessed in teamwork or in partnerships, where everyone has and owns their own voice, and where non-disabled people take support from, as well as give support to, people with intellectual disabilities. Continuing to run services that rely on underpaid, poorly trained and minimally supervised staff is simply not going to get there.

Conclusion

The cover for this book is a painting by Philip Kearney who is a disabled artist in Ireland. We chose this as the cover because it seemed an appropriate metaphor both for this book and for a good life.

The good life as we understand it involves a journey. It is a voyage of discovery. We begin it at birth and end it probably with our death. We each set out in small boats on unknown seas. Some of us are better sailors than others and are well equipped for travel. Some of us have sturdier boats and more provisions. The seas on which we voyage are unknown to us although they are not altogether uncharted. As we have seen in this book, many previous explorers have recorded their voyages and have noted some of the hazards and wrong turnings as well as providing some guidance along the way. We are not alone in our travels, others share our boat for varying lengths of time, offering support and assistance. And as you can see from the painting, other boats are with us. However we should remain always captain of our journey.

In our search for a good life we are truly explorers. Our destination is not known to us at the beginning of the voyage and is only slowly discovered. And although we may form ideas about what it may be as we travel, these can change with time and circumstances. Our attention is divided between the necessities of keeping our boat afloat and moving and on the learning that we acquire as we go along. The values and ideas about a good life that we acquire as we travel inform our voyage and shape its destination. In this conclusion we explore the implications of making a good life central in our consideration of, and work with, people with intellectual disabilities.

Making a good life central

In our view there are sound reasons for making a good life a central consideration in the lives of people with intellectual disabilities. Our policies and practices are currently predicated on a view that life can be better for people with intellectual disabilities, not that they can and should lead good lives. Our analysis of UK policies revealed a lack of clarity in the underlying values and principles that shape them. Too often we found that they were headed by mantras for a 'life like any other' or 'an ordinary life'. These do not supply the kind of thought-through value base that underpins a good life as formulated in Western thought and tradition. And mantras undersell the lives of people with intellectual disabilities. None of us really wants to lead 'an ordinary life' or 'a life like any other' even if we could define what this means.

A consideration of what a good life might be for individuals with intellectual disabilities moves us away from the repeated tendency in policy to see people with intellectual disabilities as a social problem to be managed according to the social and economic imperatives of the time. Since the early 20th century this has meant very different imposed views of how they should lead their lives. Institutionalisation in the early 20th century was seen as an answer to social problems that they were believed to present. Later community living and integration were promoted because of a changed view of marginalised groups, a focus on rights and a perceived economic saving in community living. Paradoxically this occurred at a time when geographical communities were becoming less strong. Now at a time when there is an emphasis on the productive individual worker/consumer there is a strong focus on people entering the workforce and living independently. Our analysis in this book reveals that many of these changes have led some people with intellectual disabilities to lead better lives. However the degree to which they remain subject to wider societal and economic imperatives has remained very much the same, with policies shaping their lives as if all people with intellectual disabilities were the same. We argue that they are a widely diverse group and that policies that may be positive for some may exclude or neglect others. So for people with multiple or severe impairments the current focus of policy may not lead to better or good lives, but leave them outside of consideration or unvalued.

We identified four recurrent themes in our analysis of a good life:

- Pleasure and virtue or duty.
- Happiness.
- Reason.
- Freedom and constraint.

We do not see these themes as exhaustive and Nussbaum's capabilities provide a more extended list that should be considered in a good life. However the themes we identified enabled us to see both why it has been so difficult for people with intellectual disabilities to achieve a good life and also the very real challenges of making this central in their lives.

We have come to the view that a good life, while an end in itself, can also be a tool either for the inclusion or exclusion of certain groups of people. Historically a perceived lack of reason was enough to exclude some groups (women, slaves and disabled people) from consideration of a good life. And this view still resonates in how people with intellectual disabilities may be positioned in our society. We argue that this is not now a valid case for exclusion from a good life. To go back to the metaphor that began the conclusion, we all require relationships in our lives to support us on our journey and a person's capacity to reflect and plan should be taken into account in considering with them what a good life might mean. This does place responsibility on those working with people with intellectual disabilities to provide the kind of relationship that will take into account the individual's strengths and needs.

A good life internally, not externally, imposed

If we make a good life central in the lives of people with intellectual disabilities, then we need to assume that creating what we think are good conditions around people is insufficient. A good life is one that emerges from within the person and as a result of their experiences, which are linked to their evolving values and their inner worlds. The failure to adequately consider how people with intellectual disabilities may think and feel about their lives can lead us to focus on a group of ephemeral and assumed pleasures or an additive view of happiness in which a job, a house and possessions are seen as sufficient.

We need to consider seriously the internal lives of people with intellectual disabilities. A home of one's own and a paid job may be the foundations on which some people build a good life. But they may not be the ones that all people would choose, any more than all of the rest of the population chooses these. Marie's life story revealed that a paid job, while seen as sufficient by those around her, did not satisfy her. Her concerns were not heard.

Our analysis of a good life suggests that the themes that comprise it are more subtle and abstract than material possessions or happiness. We fail people with intellectual disabilities when we do not take into account their own reflections, ideas and plans and when we do not consider as part of their lives issues of duty and virtue or of how freedom and constraint are enacted.

We need to provide space for people's dreams and ideas to be heard by those around them. As discussed earlier in this book, life histories and stories can help us to do this if we hear them. And they are not restricted to only those who can articulate verbally. We now have means and tools available to us to provide this kind of space with support for those with more severe impairments.

We do not have all the answers for how we can work with people so that good lives can emerge as a result of their active agency. But we think a first step is to provide the space to listen.

Considering *all* of the themes

We need to consider all of the possible themes that can make up a good life. As we discussed earlier in the book, we were concerned at the failure to seriously and explicitly consider themes of virtue and duty in the lives of people with intellectual disabilities. We wonder what would happen if we took Nussbaum's capability list and made it the focus of our work with people with intellectual disabilities. We do not consider easily issues of 'play', of adult responsibilities or of imagination in our work with people.

Having some guidance about a good life is in our view a positive starting point. Further, the issue of a good life is something that affects all of us. We are not here dealing with a specific set of features that only apply to people with intellectual disabilities. A focus on what a good life might mean goes some way to blurring that divide between those who are perceived as 'disabled' and those who are not.

Education for a good life

For some people with intellectual disabilities there has been a failure to provide the kind of education that would enable them to begin to shape a good life. For example, research undertaken by one of the authors in Australia with people with intellectual disabilities revealed that, for many, issues of their sexuality and relationships were either ignored or they were ruled out early in their lives by families and workers.

If virtue and duty are part of a good life, then they need to be present in the lives of people with intellectual disabilities. Yet it is just in these areas that people are most boundaried. Marie's commitment to social justice issues was not seen as central by many around her and was given less priority than the acquisition of a job.

If we place a good life as a central tenet in the lives of people with intellectual disabilities, then we need to provide them with the education and support that will enable them to create it, in company with others. The negative reactions to people with intellectual disabilities reported by their parents earlier in this book reveal that for many people a good life is ruled out from birth. Turning this culture around is difficult, but a focus on people's potential, rather than on what they cannot do, would seem to offer more avenues for choice and development.

This demands a change in the way we educate those who are close to people with intellectual disabilities; a change that places the idea of a good life centrally in their work. While in the past workers have often been seen as disempowering and oppressive by disabled people, there is a need now to value the work that personal assistants and others do and to provide them with the skills to work both respectfully and sensitively with individuals so that they are heard, as well as to take a structural view of society and take steps to look at how change might happen.

On the basis of our analysis we argue strongly for an education for all people working with people with intellectual disabilities that places the 'good life', and possible means of achieving it, at the centre of their work. This is not an argument for a workforce distanced from people with intellectual disabilities, but for a recognition that if we are to create good lives for ourselves, then we need support from those around us to do it.

Working to change the community

It is not enough to work with individuals to support them in leading a good life. There are, as the social model emphasises, real structural barriers to overcome. Bullying and the failure of our communities to support inclusion are symptomatic of broader issues that need addressing. Much more research and more action are needed to identify the reasons for such attitudes and behaviour and challenge them.

In our haste in the past to relocate people in the community we have focused very much on adapting them to fit into it. We did not provide the resources or the skills that would have supported people to belong in a community, nor did we analyse or think about what such a community might be.

We are concerned that the emphasis on inclusion does not sit easily with a view of people with intellectual disabilities as active agents creating good lives. We have taken seriously bell hooks' view about belonging because it emphasises issues of continuity, of known history and of the active engagement with others. However we are also conscious that for people with intellectual disabilities these things are difficult. There is a need at policy and practice level to consider what belonging might actually mean for people in particular communities, and to see ways in which groups that represent both their interests and concerns can be developed and maintained.

Relationships

Our metaphor indicated that we are not alone in the boat! As this book evolved it became clearer to us that the relationships that people with intellectual disabilities have with those around them are fundamental to the achievement of a good life. This is true for us all. We are now strongly of the view that the education of a workforce that is valued, and in which the difficult and subtle tasks of working to support someone in creating a good life, should be central. We still, now, in the age of personalisation, do not take seriously the kinds of experience and training that will move support workers beyond basic caring and socialising to a consideration of how people they work with may begin to lead good lives. In some ways the social model and normalisation have made it harder to develop this. Anti-professionalism has been a strong part of the disability movement and, given the past, one can see why. However it is now time to move on and to explore how workers can receive education that will support people in positive ways to lead good lives.

Finally ...

Sigmund Freud commented that the meaning of life is work and love. Broadly interpreted as a life having meaning and close relationships, this seems a good position from which to begin to work with people with learning disabilities as active agents in creating their own good lives.

Bibliography

AAMR (American Association on Mental Retardation) (2002) *Mental retardation. Definition, classification and systems of supports.* Washington: American Association on Mental Retardation.

Abberley, P. (2002) 'Work, disability, disabled people and European social theory', in C. Barnes, L. Barton and M. Oliver (eds) *Disability studies today.* Cambridge: Polity Press.

Abbott, P. and Sapsford, R. (1987) *Community care for mentally handicapped children.* London: Croom Helm.

Abbot, P. and Sapsford, R. (1997) *Research into practice.* Milton Keynes: Open University Press.

Abbott, D. and Howarth, J. (2005) *Secret loves, hidden lives? Exploring issues for men and women with learning difficulties who are gay, lesbian or bisexual.* Bristol: The Policy Press.

Aird, G., Dale, A., Edgecumbe, S., Jones, L., Rowden, T., Sabine, M., Tyler, A., Waight, M. and Wornham, S. (2009) 'Access all areas: We are VIPs', in J. Seale and M. Nind (eds) *Understanding and promoting access for people with learning difficulties.* London: Routledge.

Alice (1999) 'Alice in Wonderland. My life', in D. Atkinson et al (eds) *Good times, bad times.* Kidderminster: BILD.

Ames, T. and Samowitz, P. (1995) 'Inclusionary standards for determining sexual consent for individuals with developmental disabilities', *Mental Retardation* 33(4): 264–7.

Arthur, A. (2003) 'The emotional lives of people with learning disability', *British Journal of Learning Disabilities,* 31(1): 25–30.

Aspis, S. (1997) 'Self-advocacy for people with learning difficulties: Does it have a future?', *Disability & Society,* 14(4): 647–54.

Aspis, S. (2000) 'Researching our history: Who is in charge?', in L. Brigham, D. Atkinson, M. Jackson, S. Rolph and J. Walmsley (eds) *Crossing boundaries: Change and continuity in the history of learning disability.* Kidderminster: BILD.

Aspis, S. (2001) email debate, *Danmail,* 20 April 2001, 11:11 pm.

Atkinson, D. (1997a) *An autobiographical approach to learning disability research.* Aldershot: Ashgate.

Atkinson, D. (1997b) 'Learning from local history: Evidence from Somerset', in D. Atkinson, M. Jackson, and J. Walmsley (eds) *Forgotten lives,* pp 107–25.

Atkinson, D. (2005) 'Narratives and people with learning disabilities', in G. Grant, P. Goward, M. Richardson and P. Ramcharan (eds) *Learning disability: A life cycle approach to valuing people*. Buckingham: Open University Press.

Atkinson, D. and Ward, L. (1987) 'Friends and neighbours: Relationships and opportunities in the community for people with a mental handicap', in N. Malin (ed) *Reassessing community care*. London: Croom Helm.

Atkinson, D., Jackson, M. and Walmsley, J. (eds) (1997) *Forgotten lives: Exploring the history of learning disability*. Kidderminster: BILD.

Australian Institute of Health and Welfare (2003) 'Aged care innovation pool dementia and disability pilot services evaluation', *Welfare Division working paper no. 41*, Canberra: AIHW.

Ayer, S. and Alaszewski, A. (1984) *Community care for the mentally handicapped: Services for mothers and their mentally handicapped children*. London: Croom Helm.

Bank-Mikkelson, N. (1980) 'Denmark', in R. Flynn and K. Nitsch (eds) *Normalisation, social integration and community services*. Baltimore, MD: University Park Press, pp 51–70.

Barnes, J. (2008) *Nothing to be frightened of*. New York, NY: Alfred A. Knopf.

Barron, S. and Kelly, C. (2006) *National intellectual disability database committee annual report 2006*. Dublin: Health Research Board.

Bates, P. and Davis, F. (2004) 'Social capital, social inclusion and services for people with learning disabilities', *Disability & Society*, 19(13).

Bauman, Z. (2001) *Community. Seeking safety in an insecure world*. Cambridge: Polity Press.

Bauman, Z. (2008) *The art of life*. Cambridge: Polity Press.

Beadle-Brown, J., Mansell, J., Whelton, B., Hutchinson, A. and Skidmore, C. (2005) *Too far to go? People with learning disabilities placed out-of-area*. Canterbury: Tizard Centre.

Bersani, H. (1998) 'From social clubs to social movement: Landmarks in the development of the international self advocacy movement', in L. Ward (ed) *Innovations in advocacy and empowerment for people with intellectual disabilities*. Chorley: Lisieux Hall, pp 59–76.

Blake Marsh, R. (1943) *Bromham House Annual Report 1943* (located in Bedfordshire County Record Office MDP 27).

Blunden, A. (2004) 'Capital investment', *Eureka Street*, 14(5): 30–1.

Blunden, R. (1980) *Individual plans for mentally handicapped people: A draft procedural guide*. Cardiff: Mental Handicap in Wales Applied Research Unit, University of Wales College of Medicine.

Blyth, C. and Gardner, A. (2007) 'We're not asking for anything special: Direct payments and the carers of disabled children', *Disability & Society*, vol 22(3), 235–49.

Blythe, T. and Gardner, H. (1990) 'A school for all intelligences', *Educational Leadership*, 47(7): 33–7.

BMRB, Lancaster University and Central England People First (2005) *English national survey of adults with learning disabilities 2003–4*. London: The Health and Social Care Information Centre.

Booth, T. and Booth, W. (1994) *Parenting under pressure: Mothers and fathers with learning difficulties*. Buckingham: Open University Press.

Booth, T. and Booth, W. (1996) 'Sounds of silence. Narrative research with inarticulate subjects', *Disability & Society*. 11(1): 55–70.

Bornat, J. (1997) 'Representations of community', in J. Bornat, J. Johnson, C. Pereira, D. Pilgrim and F. Williams (eds) *Community care: A reader*, 2nd edn. London: Palgrave Macmillan.

Bornat, J., Johnson, J., Pereira, C., Tomasini, F., Pilgirm, D. and Williams, F. (eds) (1997) *Community care: A reader*. Basingstoke: Macmillan.

Brandon, D. and Ridley, J. (1985) *Beginning to listen*. London: Campaign for People with Mental Handicaps.

Brewster, J. and Ramcharan, P. (2005) 'Enabling and supporting person centred approaches', in G. Grant, P. Goward, M. Richardson and P. Ramcharan (eds) *Learning disability: A life cycle approach to valuing people*. Buckingham: Open University Press.

Browder, D. and Cooper, K. (1994) 'Inclusion of older adults with mental retardation in leisure opportunities', *Mental Retardation* 32: 91–9.

Brown, H. and Smith, H. (eds) (1992) *Normalisation: A reader for the 90s*. London: Routledge.

Brown, I. and Brown, R. (2003) *Quality of life and disability. An approach for community practitioners*. London: Jessica Kingsley Publishers.

Buchanan, I. and Walmsley, J. (2006) 'Self advocacy in historical perspective', *British Journal of Learning Disabilities*, 34: 133–8.

Burchardt, T. (2004) 'Capabilities and disability: The capabilities framework and the social model of disability', *Disability & Society*, 19(7): 735–51.

Burton, M. and Kagan, C. (2006) 'Decoding "Valuing People". Social policy for people who are learning disabled', *Disability & Society*, 21(4): 299–313.

Campbell, J. (2006) 'Direct payments: The heart of independent living', in J. Leece and J. Bornat (eds) *Developments in direct payments*, Bristol: The Policy Press, pp 130–2.

Carpenter, M. (2009) 'The capabilities approach and critical social policy: Lessons from the majority world?', *Critical Social Policy*, 29: 351–73.

Carter, J. (1981) *Day services for adults: Somewhere to go.* London: George Allan and Unwin.

Castles, K. (2004) 'Nice, average Americans: Postwar parents' groups and the defense of the normal family', in S. Noll and J. Trent (eds) *Mental retardation in America.* New York: New York University Press.

Chadsey-Rusch, J., Linneman, D. and Rylance, B. (1997) 'Beliefs about social integration from the perspectives of persons with mental retardation, job coaches and employers', *American Journal on Mental Retardation*, 102(1): 1–12.

Changing our Lives (forthcoming) 'Our journey through time', *British Journal of Learning Disabilities*.

Chapman, R. (2005) 'The role of the self-advocacy support-worker in UK People First Groups: Developing inclusive research', Unpublished PhD thesis, Open University.

Chapman, R. and McNulty, N. (2004) 'Building bridges? The role of research support in self advocacy', *British Journal of Learning Disabilities*, 32(2): 77–85.

Chappell, A. (1992) 'Towards a sociological critique of the normalisation principle', *Disability, Handicap & Society*, 7(1): 35–51.

Chappell, A. L. (1997) 'From normalization to where?', in L. Barton and M. Oliver (eds) *Disability studies: Past, present and future*, Leeds: Disability Press, pp 45–61.

Chenoweth, L. (2000) 'Closing the doors: Insights and reflections on deinstitutionalisation', in M. Jones and L. Marks (eds) *Explorations on law and disability in Australia.* Melbourne: The Federation Press, pp 77–100.

Chesley, G. and Calaluce, P. (1997) 'The deception of inclusion', *Mental Retardation*, 35(6): 488–90.

Clapton, J. (2009) *A transformatory ethic of inclusion: Rupturing concepts of disability and inclusion.* Rotterdam: Sense Publishers.

Clarke, L. and Griffiths, P. (2008) *Learning disability and other intellectual impairment*, London: Wiley.

Clark, L. and Griffiths, P. (eds) (2008) *Learning disability and other intellectual impairments: Meeting needs through health services.* London: Wiley.

Clement, T. (2004) 'An anthropology of People First, Anytown', Unpublished PhD thesis, Open University.

Clement, T. and Bigby, C. (2010) *Group homes for people with intellectual disabilities. Encouraging inclusion and participation.* London: Jessica Kingsley Publishers.

Clement, T., Bigby, C. and Johnson, K. (2006) *Making life good in the community. The story so far.* Melbourne: Latrobe University.

Cole, P. (1999) 'The structure and arguments used to support or oppose inclusion policies for students with disabilities', *Journal of Intellectual & Developmental Disability*, 24(3): 215–26.

Coleman, J. (1988) 'Social capital in the creation of human capital', *American Journal of Sociology*, 94: S95–S120.

Concannon, L. (2005). *Planning for life.* London: Routledge.

Cooper, M. (1997) 'My life story', in D. Atkinson, M. Jackson and J. Walmsley (eds) *Forgotten lives: Exploring the history of learning disability.* Kidderminster: BILD publications.

Cottingham, J. (1998) *Philosophy and the good life. Reason and the passions in Greek, Cartesian and psychoanalytic ethics.* Cambridge: Cambridge University Press.

Cottis, T. (ed) (2009) *Intellectual disability, trauma and psychotherapy.* London: Routledge.

Cox, E. (1996) *A truly civil society.* Melbourne: ABC Books.

Croucher, K. (2005) 'Knocking the system', in S. Rolph, D. Atkinson, M. Nind and J. Welshman (eds) *Witnesses to change: Families, learning difficulties and history.* Kidderminster: BILD, pp 143–52.

Culham, A. (2003) 'Deconstructing normalisation: Clearing the way for inclusion', *Journal of Intellectual & Developmental Disability*, 28(1): 65–78.

Cummins, R. (2004) 'Service providers as managers of clients' subjective well being', *Plenary presentation IASSID*, June, Melbourne.

Dale, P. (2008) 'Review of community care in perspective', *British Journal of Learning Disabilities*, 36: 73–4.

Dalley, G. (1988) *Ideologies of caring: Rethinking community and collectivism.* London: Macmillan.

Davis, K. (2004) 'The crafting of good clients', in J. Swain, S. French, C. Barnes and C. Thomas (eds) *Disabling barriers: Enabling environments.* London: Sage, pp 203–5.

De Botton, A. (2001) *The consolations of philosophy.* London: Penguin.

Department of Human Services (2006) *About the Disability Act.* Melbourne: Victorian Government.

DH (Department of Health) (2001) *Valuing people: A new strategy for learning disability for the 21st century.* Norwich: The Stationery Office.

DH (2007a) *Putting people first. A shared commitment to the transformation of adult social care.* London: The Stationery Office.

DH (2007b) *Valuing people now. Consultation report*. London: The Stationery Office.

DH (2009) *Valuing people now*. Norwich: The Stationery Office.

DHSS (Department of Health and Social Security) (1971) *Better services for the mentally handicapped* (Cmnd 4683). London: HMSO.

DisAbility Services, Division (2000) *State DisAbility services plan*. Melbourne: Department of Human Services.

Dowse, L. (2009) '"Some people are never going to be able to do that": Challenges for people with intellectual disability in the 21st century', *Disability & Society*, 24(5): 571–84.

Duffy, S. (2006) *In control: Economics of self directed support*. London: In Control.

Eagleton, T. (2007) *The meaning of life. A very short introduction*. Oxford: Oxford University Press.

Edgerton, R. (1967) *The cloak of competence. Stigma in the lives of the mentally retarded*. Los Angeles, CA: University of California Press.

Eliot, T. S. (2004) 'Little Gidding', in T. S. Elliot, *Collected plays and poems*. London: Faber and Faber.

Emerson, E., Malam, S., Davies, I. and Spencer, K. (2005) *Adults with learning difficulties in England 2003/4*. London: Health and Social Care Information Centre.

Enable UN (2003) 'Developmental and psychiatric disabilities', www.un.org/esa/socdev/enable/disdevelopmental.htm

Felce, D. and Emerson, E. (2001) 'Living with support in a home in the community: Predictors of behavioural development and household and community activity', *Mental Retardation and Developmental Disabilities Research Review*, 7: 75–83.

Felce, D., Grant, G., Todd, S., Ramcharan, P., McGrath, M., Perry, J. and Kilsby, M. (1998) *Towards a full life: Researching policy innovation for people with learning disabilities*, London: Butterworth-Heinemann.

Finlay, W., Walton, C. and Antaki, C. (2008) 'Promoting choice and control in residential services for people with learning disabilities', *Disability & Society*, 23(4): 349–60.

Firth, H. and Rapley, M. (1990) *From acquaintance to friendship: Issues for people with learning disabilities*. Kidderminster: BILD.

Fisher, D. (1999) 'According to their peers: Inclusion as high school students see it', *Mental Retardation*, 37(6): 458–67.

Fleet, C. and Johnson, D. (2002) *Clients with complex care needs: Implications for planned activity groups (high) service delivery*. Melbourne: Bundoora Extended Care.

Foundation for People with Learning Difficulties (2009) 'Statistics about people with learning disabilities', www.learningdisabilities.org. uk/information/learning-disabilities-introduction/

French, C. (1971) *A history of the development of the mental health service in Bedfordshire 1948-1970*, Bedford: Bedfordshire County Council Health Committee.

French S (1993) 'What's so great about independence?', in J. Swain, v. Finkelstein, S. French and M. Oliver (eds) *Disabling barriers. Enabling environments*, London:Sage

French, S. (2004) 'Can you see the rainbow? The roots of denial', in J. Swain, S. French, C. Barnes and C. Thomas (eds) *Disabling barriers: Enabling environments.* London: Sage.

Freud, S. and Strachey, J. (2001) *The complete psychological works of Sigmund Freud. The ego and the id and other works* (Vol 19). London: Penguin.

Fyffe, C., Johnson, K. and Bigby, C. (2005) 'Making life good in the community. Quality of Life', Unpublished Paper, Melbourne.

Gardner, H. (1990) *Frames of mind. The theory of emotional intelligence.* New York, NY: Basic Books/Simon and Schuster.

Gibson, B., Brooks, D., De Matteo, D. and King, A. (2009) 'Consumer directed personal assistance and "care": Perspectives of workers and ventilator users', *Disability & Society*, 24(3): 317–30.

Giddens, A. (1991) *Modernity and self identity. Self and society in the late modern age.* Stanford: Stanford University Press.

Gilligan, C. (1991) *In a different voice. Psychological theory and women's development.* Harvard: Harvard University Press.

Gilligan, C. and Richards, D. (2009) *The deepening darkness. Patriarchy, resistance and the future of democracy.* New York, NY: Cambridge University Press.

Glasby, G., Glendinning, C. and Littlechild, R. (2006) 'The future of direct payments', in J. Leese and J. Bornat (eds) *Developments in direct payments.* Bristol: The Policy Press.

Goffman, E. (1968) *Asylums. Essays on the social situation of mental patients and other patients.* Harmondsworth: Penguin.

Goffman, E. (1990) *Stigma. Notes on the management of a spoiled identity.* Harmondsworth: Penguin.

Goldmeyer, J. and Herr, S. (1999) *Empowerment and inclusion in planning.* Baltimore: Brookes.

Goodley, D. (2000) *Self-advocacy in the lives of people with learning difficulties.* Buckingham: Open University Press.

Goodley, D and Ramcharan, P (2005) Advocacy, campaigning and people with learning difficulties', in G. Grant, P. Goward, M. Richardson and P. Ramcharan (eds) *Learning disability: A life cycle approach to valuing people,* Buckingham: Open University Press.

Grant, G. and Ramcharan, P. (2005) 'Making a life in the community: Is intensive personalised support enough?', in G. Grant, P. Goward, M. Richardson and P. Ramcharan (eds) *Learning disability: A life cycle approach to valuing people,* Buckingham: Open University Press.

Grant, G., McGrath, M. and Ramcharan, P. (1995) 'Community inclusion of older adults with learning disabilities. Care in place', *International journal of network and community,* 2(1): 29–44.

Gray, B. and Jackson, R. (eds) (2002) *Advocacy and learning disability.* London: Jessica Kingsley.

Grayling, A. (2003) *What is good? The search for the best way to live.* London: Phoenix.

Grayling, A. (2007) *The choice of Hercules. Pleasure, duty and the good life in the 21st century.* London: Phoenix.

Griffin, J. (2007) *On human rights.* Oxford: Oxford University Press.

Grover, R. (2007) 'Foreword', in N. Wood and S. Paget (eds) *Services standards for communities with people with learning difficulties.* London: R. C. Psych.

Hagner, D., Helm, D. and Butterworth, J. (1996) 'This is your meeting. A qualitative study of person-centred planning', *Mental Retardation,* 34(3): 159–71.

Harris, R. (2005) 'I don't think I'll give up till I die', in S. Rolph, D. Atkinson, M. Nind and J. Welshman (eds) *Witnesses to change: Families, learning difficulties and history,* Kidderminster: BILD, pp 47–54.

Hatton, C. (2008) *A report on In Control's second phase: Evaluation and learning 2005–7.* London: In Control. www.in-control.org.uk/site/INCO/UploadedResources/0550_Phase_Two_Report.pdf.pdf

Healthcare Commission (2005) *Joint investigation into services for people with learning disabilities in Cornwall NHS Partnership Trust.* London: Healthcare Commission.

Healthcare Commission (2007) *Investigation into service for people with learning disabilities provided by Sutton and Merton Primary Care Trust.* London: Healthcare Commission.

Hobbes, T. (1969) *Leviathan.* London: The Fontana Library.

hooks, b. (2009) *Belonging.* New York, NY: Routledge.

House of Lords/House of Commons Joint Committee on Human Rights (2008) *A life like any other. Human rights of adults with learning disabilities* (vols 1 and 2). London: The Stationery Office.

Hughes, C., Kim, J. and Hwang, B. (1998) 'Assessing social integration in employment settings: Current knowledge and future directions', *American journal on Mental Retardation*, 103(2): 173–85.

Humber, L. (forthcoming) 'Getting a job: Theorising the work experiences of learning-disabled young people', unpublished PhD thesis, Milton Keynes, Open University.

Inclusion International (2005) *Inclusion International Strategic Plan*, www.inclusion-international.org/priorities/strategic-plan/

Ingham, N. (forthcoming) 'End of an era: An oral history of the closure of the Royal Albert Hospital, Lancaster', unpublished PhD thesis, Milton Keynes: Open University.

Jackson, M. (2001) *The borderland of imbecility: Medicine, society and the fabrication of the feeble mind in late Victorian and Edwardian England*. Manchester: Manchester University Press.

Jay, P. (1979) *Report of the Committee of Enquiry into Mental Handicap Nursing and Care* (Cmnd 7468). London: HMSO.

Johnson, K. (1998) *Deinstitutionalising women. An ethnographic study of institutional closure*. Melbourne: Cambridge University Press.

Johnson, K. (2006) '16 Temple Court: A description', in T. Clement, C. Bigby and K. Johnson (eds) *Making life good in the community. The story so far*. Melbourne: Department of Human Services.

Johnson, K. (2009) 'No longer researching about us without us. A researcher's reflection on rights and inclusive research in Ireland', *British Journal of Learning Disabilities*, 37(4): 250–6.

Johnson, K. and Bigby, C. (2005) 'Making life good in the community. What is action research?', Unpublished Discussion Paper.

Johnson, K. and Tait, S. (2003) 'Throwing away the key: People with intellectual disabilities and involuntary detention', in I. Freckleton and K. Diesfeld (eds) *Involuntary detention and civil commitment: International perspectives*. London: Bloomesbury.

Johnson, K. and Traustadottir, R. (2005) *Deinstitutionalization and people with intellectual disabilities. In and out of institutions*. London: Jessica Kingsley Publishers.

Johnson, K., Hillier, L. and Harrison, L. (2001) *People with intellectual disabilities. Living safer sexual lives*. Melbourne: Latrobe University.

Jones, G. (1986) *Social hygiene in twentieth century Britain*. London: Croom Helm.

Jones, K. (1960) *Mental health and social policy 1845–1959*. London: Routledge and Kegan Paul.

Jones, K. (2004) 'Education for children with mental retardation: Parent activism, public policy and family ideology in the 1950s', in S. Noll and J. Trent (eds) *Mental retardation in America*. New York: New York University Press.

Kearney, P. with Johnson, K. (2009) *This was my life: I'm here to tell it: The life and times of Patrick Kearney*. Ennis: Clare Inclusive Research Group.

King's Fund (1980) *An ordinary life*. London: King's Fund.

Kliewer, C. (1998) 'The meaning of inclusion', *Mental Retardation*, 36(4): 317–21.

Klotz, J. (2004) 'Socio-cultural study of intellectual disability: Moving beyond labelling and social constructionist perspectives', *British Journal of Learning Disabilities*, 32(2): 93–104.

Kohn, M. (2008) *Self interest and the common good*. Oxford: Oxford University Press.

Korman, R. and Petronko, M. (2004) 'Community inclusion of individuals with behavioural challenges: Who supports caregivers?', *Mental Retardation*, 42(3): 223–8.

Kuhse, H. and Singer, P. (2002) 'Should all seriously disabled infants live?', in H. Kuhse and P. Singer (eds) *Unsanctifying human life*. Oxford: Blackwell Publishing, pp 233–45.

Ladurie, Le Roy (1990) *Montaillou*. London: Penguin.

Lancaster University (2007) 'Results published for the first national survey of adults with learning difficulties in England 2003/04', Press release, www.lancs.ac.uk/fass/ihr/research/learning/projects/natsurvey.htm

Lasch, C. (1995) *The revolt of the elites and the betrayal of democracy*. New York: W.W. Norton and Co.

Lecomte, J. and Mercier, C. (2009) 'The emergence of the human rights of persons with intellectual disabilities in international law: The cases of the Montreal declaration on intellectual disabilities and the UN Convention on the Rights of Persons with Disabilities', in F. Owen and D. Griffiths (eds) *Challenges to the human rights of people with intellectual disabilities*. London: Jessica Kingsley Publishers, pp 43–75.

Ledger, S. (in progress) 'Staying local: Life stories from inner London', Unpublished PhD, Milton Keynes: Open University.

Leece, J. (2006) 'It's not like being at work: A study to investigate stress and job satisfaction in employees of direct payments users', in J. Bornat and J. Leece (eds) *Developments in direct payments*, Bristol: The Policy Press, pp 189–204.

Leece, J. and Bornat, J. (eds) (2006) *Developments in direct payments*, Bristol: The Policy Press.

Lindley, P. and Wainwright, T. (1992) 'Normalisation training: Conversion or commitment?', in H. Brown and H. Smith (eds) *Normalisation: A reader for the nineties.* London: Routledge, pp 19–34.

Locke, J. ([1690] 1988) *Two treatises on government*, edited by P. Laslett, Cambridge: Cambridge University Press.

London People Available at www.peoplefirstltd.com/index.php

Lord, J. and Hutchinson, P. (2003) 'Individualised support and funding: Building blocks for capacity building and inclusion', *Disability & Society*, 18(1): 71–86.

McCallion, P., Janicji, M. and Kolomer, S. (2004) 'Controlled evaluation of support groups for grandparent caregivers for children with developmental disabilities and delays', *American Journal on Mental Retardation*, 109(5): 352–61.

McConkey, R. (2005) 'Promoting friendships and developing social networks', in G. Grant, P. Goward, M. Richardson and P. Ramcharan (eds) *Learning disability: A life cycle approach to valuing people.* Buckingham: Open University Press.

McConkey, R. and Collins, S. (2009) 'Promoting social inclusion through building bridges and bonds', in J. Seale and M. Nind (eds) *Understanding and promoting access for people with learning difficulties.* London: Routledge.

McDonagh, P. (2008) *Idiocy: A cultural history*, Liverpool: Liverpool University Press.

McFadden, M. (2002) 'Testimony from M. McFadden and R. McKenzie', in *Lennox Castle exhibition: The human history of an institution* (exhibition booklet).

McKenzie R. (2002) 'Testimony from M. McFadden and R. McKenzie', in *Lennox Castle exhibition: The human history of an institution* (exhibition booklet).

McMahon, D. (2006) *Happiness a history.* New York, NY: Grove Press.

Mack, T. (2001) 'We'll do it our way', *Guardian Weekend*, 14 April.

Malin, N., Race, D., and Jones, G. (1980) *Services for the mentally handicapped in Britain*, London: Croom Helm.

Mansell, J. (2003) 'My home – your workplace. The tension, the challenge', *Keynote address, NACS conference*, Melbourne.

Martin, J. (1984) *Hospitals in trouble.* Oxford: Basil Blackwell.

Maslow, A. (1969) *Towards a psychology of being.* New York, NY: John Wiley and Sons.

Means, R., Richards, S. and Smith, R. (2003) *Community care: Policy and practice* (3rd edn). London: Palgrave.

Metzel, D. (2004) 'Historical social geography', in S. Noll and J.W. Trent (eds) *Mental retardation in America*. New York: New York University Press, pp 420–44.

Meyer, M., Donelly, M. and Weerakoon, P. (2007) 'They're taking the place off my hands: Perspectives of people using personal care', *Disability & Society*, 22(6): 595–608.

Michaels, J. (2008) *Health care for all. Independent inquiry into access to healthcare for people with learning disabilities*. London: Department of Health.

Millear, A. with Johnson, K. (2000) '39 months under the Disability Discrimination Act', in R. Traustadottir and K. Johnson (eds) *Women with intellectual disabilities. Finding a place in the world*. London: Jessica Kingsley Publishers, pp 239–52.

Milton, J. ([1674] 2005) *Paradise lost. An illustrated edition with an introduction by Philip Pullman*. Oxford: Oxford University Press.

MIND (1971) *Report No. 1*. London: National Association for Mental Health.

Mitchell, D. (2006) 'Review of *Witnesses to change*', *British Journal of Learning Disabilities*, 34(2): 124–7.

Mitchell, D. and Welshman, J. (2006) 'In the shadow of the poor law: Workforce issues', in J. Welshman and J. Walmsley (eds) *Community care in perspective*, London: Palgrave.

Mitra, S. (2006) 'The capability approach and disability', *Journal of disability policy studies*, 16(4): 236–47.

Moore, C., Harley, D. and Gamble, D. (2004) 'Ex-post-facto analysis of competitive employment outcomes for individuals with mental retardation: National perspective', *Mental Retardation*, 42(4): 253–62.

Morris, J. (1993) 'Independent living and community care', *Critical Social Policy*, 14(40): 24–45.

Morris, J. (2004) 'Review of *Witnesses to change*', *British Journal of Learning Disabilities*, 34(3): 124–7.

Morris, P. (1969) *Put Away*. London: Routledge and Kegan Paul.

Mr and Mrs York (2005) 'Fight for your child', in S. Rolph, D. Atkinson, M. Nind and J. Welshman (eds) *Witnesses to change: Families, learning difficulties and history*, Buckingham: Open University Press, pp 165–6.

Murdoch, I. (1993) *Metaphysics as a guide to morals*. London: Penguin.

National Council on Disability (2008) *Finding the gaps. A comparative analysis of disability laws in the United States to the United Nations Convention on the Rights of Persons with Disabilities (CRPD)*. Washington: National Council on Disability.

National Statistics and NHS Health and Social Care Information Centre (2005) *Adults with learning difficulties in England 2003/4*, London: DH.

NCCL (UK National Council for Civil Liberties) (1951) *50,000 Outside the law: An examination of the treatment of those certified as mental defectives*. London: NCCL.

Nickson, B. (2005) 'Never take no for an answer', in S. Rolph, D. Atkinson, M. Nind and J. Welshman (eds) *Witnesses to change: Families, learning difficulties and history*. Buckingham: Open University Press, pp 77–86.

Niedecken, D. (2003) *Nameless: Understanding learning disability.* London: Brunner-Routledge.

Nolan, M., Grant, G., Keady, J. and Lundh, U. (2003) 'New directions for partnerships: Relationship centred care', in M. Nolan, U. Lundh, G. Grant and J. Keady (eds) *Partnerships in family care: Understanding the care giver*. Berkshire: Open University Press.

Noll, S. and Trent, J. W. Jr. (eds) (2004) *Mental retardation in America.* New York, NY: New York University Press.

Nussbaum, M. (2000) *Women and human development.* Cambridge: Cambridge University Press.

Nussbaum, M. (2001a) 'Adaptive preferences and women's options', *Economics and Philosophy*, 17: 67–88.

Nussbaum, M. (2001b) *The intelligence of emotions.* Cambridge: Cambridge University Press.

Nussbaum, M. (2006) *Frontiers of justice. Disability nationality species membership*. Cambridge: Harvard University Press.

O'Brien, J. and Lyle, C. (1987) *Frameworks for accomplishments: A workshop for people developing better services.* Decatur, Georgia: Responsive Systems Associates.

O'Connor, M. (2008) 'Community', *The Guardian*, 27 December.

O'Connor, N. and Tizard, J. (1954) 'A survey of patients in twelve mental deficiency institutions', *British Medical Journal*, i: 16–18.

O'Connor, N. and Tizard, J. (1956) *The social problem of mental deficiency*, London: Pergamon Press.

Oliver, M. (1990) *The politics of disablement*, London: Macmillan.

Oliver, M. (1996) *Understanding disability. From theory to practice.* London: Macmillan.

Oliver, M. and Barnes, C. (1998) *Disabled people and social policy. From exclusion to inclusion.* London: Longman.

Owen, F., Griffiths, D., Tarulli, D. and Murphy, J. (2009) 'Historical and theoretical foundations of the rights of persons with intellectual disabilities: Setting the stage', in F. Owen and D. Griffiths (eds) *Challenges to the human rights of people with intellectual disabilities*. London: Jessica Kingsley Publishers, pp 23–42.

Palmer, N., Peacock, C., Turner, F. and Vasey, B. supported by Williams, V. (1999) 'Telling people what you think', in J. Swain and S. French (eds) *Therapy and learning difficulties*. London: Butterworth Heinemann, pp 33–46.

Park, D. and Radford, J. (1998) 'From the case files: Reconstructing a history of involuntary sterilization', *Disability & Society*, 13(3): 317–42.

Parmenter, T. (2001) 'The contribution of science in facilitating the inclusion of people with intellectual disability into the community', *Journal of intellectual developmental disability*, 45(3): 183–93.

Pawson, N., Raghavan, R., Small, N., Craig, S. and Spencer, M. (2005) 'Social inclusion, social networks, ethnicity: The development of the social inclusion interview schedule for young people with learning disabilities', *British Journal of Learning Disabilities*, 33(1): 15–22.

Perrin, B. and Nirje, B. (1989) 'Setting the record straight: A critique of some frequent misconceptions of the normalisation principle', in A. Brechin and J. Walmsley (eds) *Making connections. Reflecting on the lives and experiences of people with learning difficulties*. London: Hodder and Stoughton, pp 220–8.

Plato (1966) 'Book VII (Allegory of the cave)', in I. A. Richards (ed and trans) *Plato's Republic*. Cambridge: Cambridge University Press.

Prideaux, S., Roulstone, A., Harris, J. and Barnes, C. (2009) 'Disabled people and self-directed support schemes: Reconceptualising work and welfare in the 21st century', *Disability & Society*, 24(5): 557–69.

Prieger, A. (2004) 'Make it as normal as possible with humor', *Mental Retardation*, 42(6): 427–44.

Putnam, R. (2000) *Bowling alone. The collapse and revival of American community*. New York, NY: Simon and Schuster.

Quinn, G. (2009) 'Bringing the UN Convention on Rights for Persons with Disabilities to life in Ireland', *British Journal of Learning Disabilities*, 37(4): 245–50.

Ramcharan, P. and Grant, G. (2001) 'Views and experiences of people with intellectual disabilities and their families: 1. The user perspective', *Journal of applied research in intellectual disabilities*, 14: 348–63.

Ramcharan, P., Roberts, G., Grant, G. and Borland, J. (2002) *Empowerment in everyday life*. London: Jessica Kingsley.

Rapley, M. (2003a) *The social construction of intellectual disability*. Cambridge: Cambridge University Press.

Rapley, M. (2003b) *Quality of life research. A critical introduction.* London: Sage.

Rawls, J. (1999) *A theory of justice* (revised edition). Oxford: Oxford University Press.

Read, J. and Walmsley, J. (2006) 'Historical perspectives on special education 1890–1970', *Disability & Society*, 21(5): 455–69.

Reaume, G. (2004) 'No profits, just a pittance: Work, compensation and people defined as mentally disabled in Ontario 1964–1990', in S. Noll and J. Trent (eds) *Mental retardation in America*, New York: New York University Press.

Redley, M. (2008) 'Citizens with learning disabilities and the right to vote', *Disability & Society*, 23(4): 375–84.

Redley, M. (2009) 'Understanding the social exclusion and stalled welfare of citizens with learning disabilities', *Disability & Society*, 24(4): 489–501.

Redley, M. and Weinberg, D. (2007) 'Learning disability and the limits of liberal citizenship: Interactional impediments to the political empowerment', *Sociology of Health and Illness*, 29(5): 767–86.

Reinders, J. (2002) 'The good life for citizens with intellectual disability', *Journal of intellectual disability research*, 46(1): 1–5.

Reynolds, J., Muston, R., Heller, T., Leach, J., McCormick, M., Wallcraft, J. and Walsh, M. (2009) *Mental health still matters.* London: Palgrave Macmillan.

Richardson, A. and Ritchie, J. (1989) *Developing friendships, enabling people with learning difficulties to make and maintain friends.* London: The Policy Institute.

Riddell, S., Barron, S. and Wilson, A. (1999) 'Social capital and people with learning difficulties', *Studies in the education of adults*, 31: 49–60.

Rivera, G. (1972) *Willowbrook: A report on how it is and why it doesn't have to be that way.* New York: Random House.

Roberts, B. (2009) 'In conversation', *British Journal of Learning Disabilities*, 37(4): 242–5.

Robertson, J., Emerson, E., Gregory, N., Hatton, C., Kessissoglou, S. and Hallam, A. (2001) 'Social networks of people with mental retardation in residential settings', *Mental Retardation*, 39: 201–14.

Roeher Institute (1995) *Research issues in evaluating deinstitutionalisation: A review of the literature.* Toronto: Roeher Institute.

Roeher Institute (1999) *Labor force inclusion of parents caring for children with disabilities.* Ontario, Canada: Roeher Institute.

Rolph, S. (2000) 'The history of community care for people with learning difficulties in Norfolk 1930–1980: The role of two hostels', Unpublished PhD thesis, Milton Keynes: Open University.

Rolph, S. (2002) *Reclaiming the past: The role of local Mencap Societies in the development of community care in East Anglia.* Milton Keynes: Open University.

Rolph, S. (2005a) *A little glamour with a strict tempo: The history of Cambridge Mencap* (vol 1, 1947–1990). Milton Keynes: Open University.

Rolph, S. (2005b) *A hidden heritage: Local Mencap Societies and the provision of social care in East Anglia, 1946–1990.* Milton Keynes: The Open University.

Rolph, S. and Atkinson, D. (forthcoming) 'The role of emotion in narrating the history of learning disability', *Oral History*.

Rolph, S. and Walmsley, J. (2001) 'The development of community care for people with learning difficulties 1913–1946', *Critical Social Policy*, 21(1): 59–80.

Rolph, S. and Walmsley, J. (2006) 'Oral history and new orthodoxies: Narrative accounts in the history of intellectual disability', *Oral History*, 34(1): 81–91.

Rolph, S., Atkinson, D., Nind, M. and Welshman, J. (eds) (2005) *Witnesses to change: Families, learning difficulties and history.* Kidderminster: BILD Publications.

Rose, N. (1979) 'The psychological complex: Mental measurement and social administration', *Ideology and consciousness*, 5: 5–68.

Rose, N. (2000) *Powers of freedom.* Cambridge: Cambridge University Press.

Rothman, D. and Rothman, R. (1984) *The Willowbrook wars.* New York, NY: Harper and Row.

Roulstone, A. (2000) 'Disability, dependency and the new deal for disabled people', *Disability & Society*, 15(3): 427–45.

Rousseau, J.-J. (1996) *The social contract.* Hertfordshire: Wordsworth Editions.

Russell, D. (2005) *Plato on pleasure and the good life.* Oxford: Oxford University Press.

Ryan, J. with Thomas, F. (1980) *The politics of mental handicap.* Harmondsworth: Penguin.

Ryan, J. with Thomas, F. (1987) *The politics of mental handicap*, revised edn, London: Free Association Books.

Sandel, M. (2009) *Justice. What's the right thing to do?* London: Penguin.

Sanderson, H. (1995) 'Self-advocacy and inclusion: Supporting people with profound and multiple disabilities', in T. Philpot and L. Ward (eds) *Values and visions: Changing ideas in services for people with learning disabilities.* Oxford: Butterworth-Heinemann, pp 244–61.

Schalock, R. and Alonso, M. (2002) *Handbook on quality of life for human services practitioners*. Washington: AAMR.

Schelley, D. (2008) 'Problems associated with choice and quality of life for an individual with intellectual disability: A personal assistant's reflexive ethnography', *Disability & Society*, 23(7): 719–32.

SCIE (Social Care Institute for Excellence) (2008) *Commissioning person-centred, cost-effective local support for people with learning disabilities. Knowledge Review 20*. London: SCIE.

SCIE (2009) *Personalisation and learning disability: A review of evidence on advocacy and its practice for people with learning disabilities and high support needs*. London: SCIE.

Scull, A. (1984) *Decarceration. Community treatment and the deviant. A radical view* (2nd revised and enlarged edn). Oxford: Polity Press.

Seale, J. and Nind, M. (eds) (2009) *Understanding and promoting access for people with learning difficulties*. London: Routledge.

Sen, A. (1992) *Inequality reexamined*. Oxford: Oxford University Press.

Sen, A. (2009) *The idea of justice*. London: Allen Lane.

Lucius Annasus Seneca (1928-1935) *Moral essays*, Translated by J.W. Basore. Loeb Classical Library, London: William Heinemann.

Senge, P. (2006) *The fifth discipline: The art and practice of the learning organization*. New York: Doubleday/Currency.

Shakespeare, T. (2003) 'Having come so far, where to now?', *Times Higher Education Supplement*, 7 November, p 28.

Shakespeare, T. (2006) *Disability rights and wrongs*. Abingdon: Routledge.

Shakespeare, T., Gillespie-Sells, K. and Davies, D. (1996) *The sexual politics of disability: Untold desires*. London: Cassell.

Sheldon, A., Traustadottir, R., Beresford, P., Boxall, K. and Oliver, M. (2007) 'Review symposium: Disability rights and wrongs', *Disability & Society*, 22(3): 209–34.

Shennan, V. (1980) *Our concern: The story of the National Association for Mentally Handicapped Children and Adults 1946–1980*. London: The National Association for Mentally Handicapped Children and Adults.

Simeonsson, R. (1994) *Risk, resilience and prevention: Promoting the well-being of all children*. Baltimore: Brookes.

Simons, K. (1992) *Sticking up for yourself: Self advocacy and people with learning difficulties*. London: Community Care publications in association with the Joseph Rowntree Foundation.

Simons, K. (1993) *Citizen advocacy: The inside view*. Bristol: Norah Fry Research Centre.

Simons, K. (1998) *Home, work and inclusion*. Layerthorpe, York: Joseph Rowntree Foundation.

Sinason, V. (1992) *Mental handicap and the human condition*. London: Tavistock.

Sinason, V. (2003) 'Foreword' in D. Niedecken, *Nameless: Understanding learning disability*, London: Routledge, pp xvi–xvii.

Singer, P. (1993) *How are we to live? Ethics in an age of self-interest*. Melbourne: Random House.

Singer, P. and Kuhse, E. (eds) (2002) *Unsanctifying human life. Essays on ethics*. Oxford: Oxford University Press.

Skills for Care (2007) *National survey of care workers: Final report*. London: SCIE.

Slattery, J. with Johnson, K. (2000) 'Family, marriage, friends and work: This is my life', in R. Traustadottir and K. Johnson (eds) *Women with intellectual disabilities. Finding a place in the world*. London: Jessica Kingsley, pp 90–105.

Smyth, M. and McConkey, R. (2003) 'Future aspirations of parents and students with severe learning difficulties on leaving special schooling', *British Journal of Learning Disabilities*, 31(2): 54–9.

Snyder, S. and Mitchell, D. (2006) *Cultural locations of disability*. Chicago: Chicago University Press.

Social Care Workforce Unit (2008) *Lessons from outsourcing adult social care: The workforce issues*. London: Improvement and Development Agency.

Spedding, F., Harkness, E., Townson, L., Docherty, A., McNulty, N. and Chapman, R. (2002) 'The role of self advocacy: Stories from a Self Advocacy Group through the experiences of its members', in B. Gray and R. Jackson (eds) *Advocacy and learning disability*. London: Jessica Kingsley.

Stainton, T. (1994) *Autonomy and social policy: Rights, mental handicap and community care*, Aldershot: Avebury.

Stainton, T. (2000) '"Equal citizens": The discourse of liberty and rights in the history of learning disability', in L. Brigham, D. Atkinson, M. Jackson, S. Rolph and J. Walmsley (eds) *Crossing boundaries: Change and continuity in the history of learning disability*. Kidderminster: BILD Publications.

Stainton, T. (2006) 'The evolution of community living in Canada: Ontario 1945–2005', in J. Welshman and J. Walmsley (eds) *Community care in perspective*. London: Palgrave, pp 235–45.

Stainton, T. and Boyce, P. (2004) 'I have got my life back: Users' experiences of direct payments', *Disability & Society*, 19(5), 443–54.

Stainton, T. and Boyce, S. (2008) 'Users' experience of direct payments', in J. Johnson and C. De Souza (eds) *Understanding health and social care: An introductory reader* (2nd edn). London: Sage/Open University, pp 65–70.

Stone, W., Gray, M. and Hughes, J. (2003) *Social capital at work*. Melbourne: Australian Institute of Family Studies.

Taylor, S. and Bogdan, R. (1989) 'On accepting relationships between people with mental retardation and non disabled people: Towards an understanding of acceptance', *Disability, Handicap & Society*, 4(1): 21–36.

Thomas, C. (2007) *Sociologies of disability and illness. Contested ideas in disability studies and medical sociology*. Houndmills, Basingstoke: Palgrave Macmillan.

Ticoll, M. (1994) *Violence and people with disabilities: A review of the literature*. Ontario: Roeher Institute.

Tideman, M. (2005) 'Conquering life: The experience of the first integrated generaton', in K. Johnson and R. Traustadottir (eds) *Deinstitutionalization and people with intellectual disabilities. In and out of institutions*. London: Jessica Kingsley Publishers, pp 211–21.

Tilley, E. (2006) 'Advocacy for people with learning difficulties: The role of two organisations', Unpublished PhD thesis, Open University, Milton Keynes.

Titmuss, R. (1961) 'Care – or cant?', *Spectator*, 17 March, pp 854–6.

Titmuss, R. (1971) *The gift relationship. From blood to social policy*. New York, NY: Pantheon.

Tizard, J., and O'Connor, N. (1952) 'The occupational adaptation of high-grade mental defectives', *Lancet*, 2 (6735): 620–3.

Tombs, A. and Tombs, M. (2005) 'A life of campaigning', in S. Rolph, D. Atkinson, M. Nind and J. Welshman (eds) *Witnesses to change: Families, learning difficulties and history*. Kidderminster: BILD, pp 277–86.

Tøssebro, J. (2005), 'Reflections on living outside: Continuity and change in the life of "outsiders"', in K. Johnson and R. Traustadottir (eds) *Deinstitutionalisation and people with intellectual disabilities*, chapter 16.

Tøssebro, J. (2006) 'The development of community services for people with learning disabilities in Norway and Sweden', in J. Welshman and J. Walmsley (eds) *Community care in perspective*. London: Palgrave.

Tøssebro, J., Gustavsson, A. and Dyrendahl, G. (eds) (1996) *Intellectual disabilities in the Nordic welfare states*. Norway: Hoyskole Forlaget.

Townson, L., Macauley, S., Harkness, E., Chapman, R., Docherty, A. et al (2004) 'We are all in the same boat: Doing people-led research', *British Journal of Learning Disabilities*, 32(2): 72–6.

Traustadottir, R. (2006) 'Learning about self advocacy from life history: A case study from the United States', *British Journal of Learning Disabilities*, 34(3): 175–80.

Traustadottir, R. and Johnson, K. (eds) (2000) *Women with intellectual disabilities: Finding a place in the world.* London: Jessica Kingsley.

Tredgold, A. F. (1908) *Mental deficiency.* London: Balliere, Tindall & Cox.

Tredgold, A. F. (1909) 'The feeble-minded – A social danger', *Eugenics review*, 1: 97–104.

Tredgold, A. (1952) *Mental deficiency,* London: Bailliere Tindall.

Trent, J. W. Jr. (1994) *Inventing the feeble mind: A history of mental retardation in the United States.* Berkeley: University of California Press.

Trent, J. (2006) 'Intellectual disabilities in the USA from the institution to the community 1948–2001', in J. Welshman and J. Walmsley (eds) *Community care in perspective.* London: Palgrave, pp 109–21.

United Nations (2005) Convention on the Rights of Persons with Disabilities, www.un.org/disabilities/convention/conventionfull.shtml

Vardy, P. and Grosch, P. (1999) *The puzzle of ethics.* London: Fountain.

Walker, P. (2009) 'Police errors contributed to tormented mother's suicide', *The Guardian*, 29 September, p 1.

Walmsley, J. (1993) 'Contradictions in caring', *Disability, Handicap & Society*, 8(2): 129–42.

Walmsley, J. (1995) 'Gender, caring and learning disability', Unpublished PhD thesis, Open University, Milton Keynes.

Walmsley, J. (2000) 'Straddling boundaries: The changing roles of voluntary organisations, 1913–1959', in L. Brigham, D. Atkinson, M. Jackson, S. Rolph and J. Walmsley (eds) *Crossing boundaries: Change and continuity in the history of learning disability.* Kidderminster: BILD Publications.

Walmsley, J. (2001) 'Normalisation, emancipatory research and learning disability', *Disability & Society*, 16(2): 187–205.

Walmsley, J. (2004) 'Inclusive learning disability research: The (non disabled) researcher's role', *British Journal of Learning Disabilities*, 32(2): 65–7.

Walmsley, J. (2005) 'Institutionalization: A historical perspective', in K. Johnson and R. Traustadottir (eds) *Deinstitutionalization and people with intellectual disabilities. In and out of institutions.* London: Jessica Kingsley.

Walmsley, J. (2006) 'Ideology, ideas and care in the community 1971–2001', in J. Welshman and J. Walmsley (eds) *Community care in perspective.* London: Palgrave, pp 38–58.

Walmsley, J. and Johnson, K. (2003) *Inclusive research with people with intellectual disabilities.* London: Jessica Kingsley Publishers.

Walmsley, J. and Mannan, H. (2009) 'Parents as co-researchers: A participatory action research initiative involving parents of people with intellectual disabilities in Ireland', *British Journal of Learning Disabilities*, 37(4): 271–6.

Ward, L. (1989) 'For better, for worse?', in A. Brechin and J. Walmsley (eds) *Making connections*. Sevenoaks: Hodder & Stoughton, pp 188–98.

Ward, L. (1995) 'Equal citizens: Current issues for people with learning difficulties and their allies', in T. Philpot and L. Ward L (eds) *Values and visions: Changing ideas in services for people with learning difficulties*, London: Butterworth-Heinemann.

Watson, L. (2002) 'Community and individual: Two perspectives on inclusion and vulnerability', *Housing, Care and Support*, 5(2): 4–11.

Watson, L., Tarpey, M., Alexander, K. and Humphreys, C. (2003) *Supporting people: Real change? Planning housing and support for marginal groups*. Bristol: Joseph Rowntree Foundation.

Webb, T. (1999) 'Voices of people with learning difficulties', in S. French (ed) *Therapy and learning difficulties*. London: Butterworth Heinemann, pp 47–57.

Webster, C. (1996) *The health services since the War: Volume II: Government and health care: The British National Health Service 1958-1979*, London: HMSO.

Wehman, P. (1996) 'Supported employment: Inclusion for all in the workplace', in W. Stainback and S. Stainback (eds) *Confronting special education. Divergent perspectives*. Boston: Allyn and Unwin.

Welsh Office (1983) *All Wales Strategy for the development of services for mentally handicapped people*, Cardiff: Welsh Office.

Welshman, J. (2006) 'Ideology, ideas and care in the community 1971–2001', in J. Welshman and J. Walmsley (eds) *Community care in perspective*. London: Palgrave, pp 17–37.

Welshman, J. and Walmsley, J. (eds) (2006) *Community care in perspective: Care, control and citizenship*. Houndmills: Palgrave Macmillan.

Widmer, E., Kempf-Constantin, K., Robert-Tissot, C., Lanzi, F. and Galli Carminati, G. (2008) 'How central and connected am I in my family? Family-based social capital of individuals with intellectual disability', *Research in Developmental Disabilities*, 29: 176–87.

Williams, V. with West of England Centre for Inclusive Living (2007) '"It's about respect": People with learning difficulties and personal assistants', Skills for Support research study (2nd stage), Bristol: Norah Fry Research Centre, University of Bristol, wwwbristol.ac.uk/norahfry/research/completed-projects/itsaboutrespect.pdf

Wilson, A. (2003) '"Real jobs", learning difficulties and supported employment', *Disability & Society*, 18(2): 99–116.

Winance, M. (2007) 'Changes to normalization processes: From alignment to work on the norm', *Disability & Society*, 22(6): 625–38.

Winter, I. (2000) *Social capital and public policy in Australia*. Melbourne: Australian Institute of Family Studies.

Wistow, R. and Schneider, J. (2003) 'Users' views on supported employment and social inclusion: A qualitative study of 30 people in work', *British Journal of Learning Disabilities*, 31(4): 166–74.

Wolfensberger, W. (1975) *The origin and nature of our institutional models*. Syracuse: Syracuse Policy Press.

Wolfensberger, W. and Tullman, S. (1989) 'A brief outline of the principle of normalization', in A. Brechin and J. Walmsley (eds) *Making connections. Reflecting on the lives and experiences of people with learning difficulties*. London: Hodder and Stoughton, pp 210–19.

Wolfensberger, W., Nirje, B., Olshansky, S., Perske, R. and Rose, P. (1972) *The principle of normalization of human services*. Toronto: National Institute on Mental Retardation.

Wood, N. and Paget, S. (2007) *Service standards for communities for people with learning difficulties* (1st edn). London: Royal College of Psychiatrists.

World Health Organisation (2001) *International classification of functioning, disability and health (ICF)*. Geneva: WHO.

Young, I. M. (2000) *Inclusion and democracy*. Oxford: Oxford University Press.

Zifcak, S. and King, A. (2009) *Wrongs, rights and remedies. An Australian charter*. Albert Park: The Australian Collaboration.

Index